The Little Book of Music and Movement

by Judith Harries
Illustrations by Michael Evans

LITTLE BOOKS WITH BIG IDEAS

Featherstone Education
An imprint of Bloomsbury Publishing Plc

50 Bedford Square
London
WC1B 3DP
UK

1385 Broadway
New York
NY 10018
USA

www.bloomsbury.com

Bloomsbury is a registered trade mark of Bloomsbury Publishing Plc

British Library Cataloguing-in-Publication Data
A catalogue record for this book is available from the British Library.

ISBN: 978-1-4729-1272-5

Library of Congress Cataloging-in-Publication Data
A catalog record for this book is available from the Library of Congress.

1 3 5 7 9 10 8 6 4 2

Printed and bound in India by Replika Pvt. Ltd

This book is produced using paper that is made from wood grown in managed,
sustainable forests. It is natural, renewable and recyclable. The logging and
manufacturing processes conform to the environmental regulations of the country of origin.

**To view more of our titles please visit
www.bloomsbury.com**

Contents

Introduction

This Little Book provides practitioners with an extensive resource for developing young children's experience of making music and exploring movement together. It provides references to music from all around the world and in a rich variety of genres, and seeks to introduce children to many diverse ways of listening, enjoying, creating and interpreting what they hear.

Nietzsche believed that 'we listen to music with our muscles'; that the physical response to music – tapping feet, moving fingers, nodding the head, feeling the beat, keeping time and, of course, dancing – are all instinctive and should be recognised and encouraged in our young children.

However, during the average school day, children are now not moving enough. There is often too much sitting for long periods of time. Young children need more opportunities to move, crawl, roll, run, climb and spin. Shorter playtimes, over-emphasis on academic attainment levels, anxious parents, health and safety, and of course 'electronic entertainment' reduce the opportunities for children to move and express themselves freely. Tests now show that many of today's children have underdeveloped balance systems and poor core strength. They need to move more, in all directions!

The activities included in this book – games, mime, movement sequences, yoga, drama, music and dance – all provide a wealth of opportunities for practitioners to use during a movement session. They can all be managed and enjoyed by both non-specialist practitioners and music and movement specialists alike.

Links with the EYFS framework

The prime areas of learning and development

Communication and language

Listening and attention
Children listen to songs and music and are encouraged to concentrate and talk about what they hear, responding with relevant comments, questions or actions.

Understanding
Children often need to follow layers of instructions when creating movement and dance interpretations.

Speaking
Many of the music and movement activities involve drama, requiring the children to express themselves effectively with a developing awareness of an audience.

Physical development

Moving and handling
This is obviously one of the main areas of learning developed by the activities in this book. There are opportunities in all activities to show good control and coordination in large and small movements. Children develop confidence in movement in a range of ways. They negotiate different space safely, and handle a variety of equipment including musical instruments, hoops, balls, quoits, scarves, saree, parachutes, etc.

Health and self-care
These activities will encourage children to realise and understand the importance of physical exercise for good health.

Personal, social and emotional development

Self-confidence and self-awareness
There are many new activities for children to try, and the chance to talk about which they enjoy. There are opportunities to sing or speak in a familiar group, to share their ideas and to choose resources.

Managing feelings and behaviour
Being aware of acceptable behaviour and working as part of a group or class in a movement activity will help children to understand and follow rules.

Making relationships
There are many games included in the activities that encourage children to take turns and play cooperatively.

The specific areas of learning and development

Literacy

Reading

Children are given opportunities to read their names and some common words.

Mathematics

Numbers

Some counting songs and rhymes encourage children to count reliably with numbers and place them in order.

Shape, space and measures

Children use everyday language to talk about shapes, position and patterns in relation to music and movement activities.

Understanding the world

People and communities

Listening to music and recreating dances from other countries will help children to know about similarities and differences between themselves and others and among families, communities and traditions.

The world

Movement ideas focussed on different seasons and weather will help children to recognise features of their own environment and understand how environments vary from one another.

Technology

Accessing music and film online and recording music and movement activities will help children to use a range of technology.

Expressive arts and design

Exploring and using media and materials

Many activities involve songs and rhymes. Children will also make music using a range of musical instruments. They will explore different ways to move and dance in response to a huge variety of music. Many suggestions are also included for ways to explore a variety of materials, tools and techniques, experimenting with colour, design, texture, form and function.

Being imaginative

Children are encouraged to use their own ideas, thoughts and feelings in the 'Music makers' and 'Moving to music' activities – see the 'What you do' section in each chapter.

How to use this book

The book begins with some general warm ups, which can be used as a resource to prepare for any music and movement activities. Pick and choose from these as a starting point for topic-based movement and dance ideas.

There are 34 different topics included in this book, all of which are popular themes from the early years curriculum, presented in alphabetical order for the practitioner to choose from. As topics are covered during the school year, activities can be selected to suit the requirements of each setting and the length of time available.

Each topic includes cross-references to other related themes, which are referred to under the chapter title, and begins with a list of 'What you need'. This is followed by 'What you do' which, as mentioned earlier, is divided into 'Music makers' – simple ideas for music activities based on the topic and suitable for all – and 'Moving to music' – several movement ideas involving a variety of music extracts and styles of movement. These do not all have to be followed in sequence and can be selected from to suit individual needs.

Games are included for each topic and explore movement ideas in a group format – some are traditional and some are original circle, inside and outside games.

The 'Songs and music' section includes an extensive list of songs and musical excerpts, all of which can be listened to online, or purchased digitally or on CD. It is a good idea to listen to a selection of the music suggested so that the best piece can be chosen for each situation to suit the children's needs and the practitioner's learning objectives.

Finally, 'Taking it further' includes some ideas for further movement activities or suggestions for other ways to develop expressive arts skills related to each topic.

General warm ups

These ideas can be used as a starting point for any movement activity. Pick and choose a few to get all the children warmed up and ready for action. Every warm up session should include some aerobic activities to prepare the heart and warm up the muscles, as well as mobility exercises and stretching moves.

▶ Marching – high knees, swinging arms, saluting, varying speed, etc.

▶ Jogging – changing direction, varying speed, adding arm movements, etc.

▶ Skipping – forwards, backwards, circles, squares, etc.

▶ Travelling in different ways – on two, three or four limbs, sideways as crabs, with a partner, etc.

▶ Freeze – the children stop travelling when they hear the whistle, and stand still.

▶ Touch – the children travel until the practitioner shouts 'Touch knees!' Each child then finds a partner and touches their knees, or as instructed.

▶ Greetings – the children travel until the practitioner shouts 'Greetings!' They then find a partner and 'greet' them – shake hands, bow, curtsey, high 5, or make up their own!

▶ DVD – use the familiar DVD controls as instructions for changing movement – play (move around), stop (stop), rewind (backwards), fast forward (speed up), pause (jog on the spot) and eject (jump up).

Mobility exercises

▶ Turn head slowly from side to side, and nod up and down.

▶ Shrug shoulders up and down, and rotate forwards and backwards.

▶ Circle arms forwards and backwards.

▶ Clock – wide legs, arms stretched up and down (at 12 and 6 o'clock); swing arms to represent different clock times.

▶ Seesaw – arms stretched out; rock up and down.

▶ Swimming – wide legs, with breaststroke, butterfly, front crawl and backstroke arms.

Stretches

▶ Turtle – walk fingers down legs, out onto floor and on all fours, then reverse.

▶ Windscreen wipers – lie on back with feet together and legs straight, then move legs side to side.

▶ Helicopter – lie on back, hands out to the side, move right leg to right hand, then across body to left hand. Repeat with left leg.

▶ Worm – lie on tummy, place hands on floor under shoulders and push up.

▶ Cat – on all fours, stretch back up into the air.

▶ Seal – lie on tummy, drag legs, flap hands and clap together.

▶ Bear – on all fours, step with right hand and right foot, left hand and left foot.

African antics

Related themes: Africa, Around the world, Harvest, Jungles, Autumn

What you need:

▶ Recorded music or access to YouTube – see 'Songs and music'
▶ A selection of African instruments – djembe drums, mbira or kalimba (thumb pianos), wooden xylophones, cabasas, natural shakers, etc.

What you do:

Music makers

▶ Learn to sing a simple call and response song from Africa (see 'Songs and music').
▶ Let the children experiment with the African instruments.
▶ Show the children how to sit on a djembe and play a simple repeated rhythm.
▶ Sit in a circle and add the other instruments to the djembe rhythm.

Moving to music

1. Play 'Djembe Drumming'. Ask the children to tap the beat as they listen.
2. Explain that they are going to create an African Harvest dance. Stand the children in a semi circle and choose one child to stand in the centre as the leader. This should be you initially, while they are learning the dance.

3. Step from side to side in time to the beat. Sow seeds by circling arms, right, left, in a big arc in front. Keep the feet moving to the beat.

4. Stamp the right foot slowly in time to the beat four times, to stomp down the seeds. Repeat with the left foot.

5. Turn to neighbour and shake hands, link arms and walk round in a circle. Stop and form a 'circle of crops'. Lift hands to the sky and wave from side to side.

6. Make chopping movements with alternate hands to cut the crops.

7. Put both hands up to head and mime carrying a basket. Scoop up the harvested crops with one hand and pretend to throw them into a basket.

8. All the time keep stepping to the beat with both feet. Add some live drumming to the recorded music. Try wearing the African masks (see 'Taking it further') to add to the drama.

Games:

▶ Try playing a child-friendly version of Kudoda, an African game similar to Jacks. Sit a group of the children around a big bowl of small beanbags. Invite the children to take turns choosing a beanbag, throwing it into the air and trying to pick up as many other beanbags as they can with one hand before the first one drops down. The winner is the child who grabs the most beanbags.

Songs and music:

'Walking through the Jungle'

Traditional 'A Keelie Makolay', 'Soualle' and 'Kye Kye Kule'

Patsy Ford Simms 'Amani Utupe'

Ladysmith Black Mambazo 'The Lion Sleeps Tonight'

Mamady Keita and Bolokada Conde 'Djembe Drumming'

Balafon Marimba Ensemble

Steve Reich 'Nagoya Marimba'

Goldfish 'Mbira beat'

Sesame Street: 'African Alphabet' and 'African Dance'

The Best of 'Ikenga Super Stars of Africa'

Taking it further

▶ Make African masks. Show the children some images of masks online. Provide them with paper plates, paints, pipe cleaners, wool and scissors.

▶ Try making some African drums by sticking two styrofoam, plastic or cardboard cups together, bottom to bottom, and then covering the open ends with strips of electrical or masking tape. Cover the outside with papier mâché and then paint and decorate the drums.

Animal ambush

Related themes: Animals, Jungles, Africa

What you need:

▶ Recorded music or access to YouTube – see 'Songs and music'

▶ Beanie baby or soft toy monkeys

▶ Saree or small parachute

What you do:

Music makers

▶ Sing the song 'Five Little Monkeys'. Ask the children to sit in a circle and hold onto the edges of the saree. Place five beanie babies or soft toy monkeys on top of the saree. Move the saree up and down so the monkeys jump and, if possible, fall off one at a time!

Moving to music

1. Talk about how different animals move. Let the children experiment with movesfor animals and demonstrate them to the group. Can the children recognise the animals?

2. Try practising some moves for these animals: lions – stalking their prey, pouncing, stopping and roaring, lazing in the sunshine; tortoises – on all fours, extending necks out, crawling very slowly; kangaroos – jumping around, standing still, patting pouch on tummy; donkeys – on all fours, walking, trotting, refusing to budge!

3. Invite individuals to demonstrate good ideas to the group.

4. Play short excerpts from 'Carnival of the Animals' related to these four animals (lion, tortoise, kangaroo, donkey) for the children to move to.

5. Explore monkey moves – walking with long arms, knuckles on the floor, hanging from a tree with one arm, swinging from tree to tree, and so on.

6. Play the song 'Go-Go Gorilla'. Let the children move around using some monkey moves.

Games:

▶ Play 'Musical chairs' with an animal theme. Set the chairs up in a circle, back to back and invite the children to dance round them. Play the song 'Walking the Dog'. When the music stops, each child must sit on a chair.

▶ Take away one chair, so next time one child is left standing. They are allowed to choose an animal sound and movement for the others to copy as they dance around the chairs.

▶ Next round, a different child will be left standing and can choose a new animal.

Songs and music:

'I Went to the Animal Fair'

'The Animals went in Two by Two'

'Five Little Monkeys Jumping on the Bed'

Tom Paxton 'Daddy's taking us to the Zoo Tomorrow'

Sonninen 'Wedding Waltz of the Mice'

Camille Saint-Saëns 'The Carnival of the Animals: March of the Lions'

Camille Saint-Saëns 'The Carnival of the Animals: Tortoises'

Camille Saint-Saëns 'The Carnival of the Animals: Kangaroos'

Camille Saint-Saëns 'The Carnival of the Animals: Persons with Long Ears'

George Gershwin 'Walking the Dog'

Henry Mancini 'Pink Panther Theme'

The Ideals 'Go-Go Gorilla'

The Monkees 'Hey Hey We're the Monkees'

Taking it further

▶ Sing 'I Went to the Animal Fair' or 'The Animals Went in Two by Two' and act out the different animals.

▶ Use play dough or clay to make model animals.

▶ Construct lion masks using paper plates. Add multi-coloured manes made from thin strips of collage materials including ribbon, wool, coloured paper, cardboard and fabric.

Autumn leaves

Related themes: Autumn, Opposites, Weather

What you need:

▶ Recorded music or access to YouTube – see 'Songs and music'
▶ Real leaves
▶ Red, yellow, orange and brown felt leaves attached to ribbons or coloured silk scarves
▶ Saree or small parachute

What you do:

Music makers

▶ Sit the children in a circle around a saree, small parachute or large square of thin fabric. Ask them to hold it gently.

▶ Put a selection of dry autumn leaves onto the saree and move it up and down in time to the beat of this song. (to the tune of 'Hot Cross Buns', changing the final word in the third line each time):

Up and down,
Up and down,
Can you hear the leaves rustling/falling/scrunching?
Up and down.

Moving to music

1. Talk about leaves falling off the trees in autumn. Use descriptive words such as 'flutter', 'float', 'fly' and 'fall'.

2. Use a xylophone or other tuned percussion instrument and play all the notes from high to low. Do the notes sound as though they are falling down?

3. Ask the children to find a space. Can they move down from high to low as the notes fall down? Invite a child to play the falling notes for the others to move to.

4. Ask the children to sit in a circle. Play any of the other songs from 'Songs and music'.

5. Invite the children to hold their hands above their heads and let their fingers 'flutter' down to the floor. Then ask them to lift their arms up and make them 'float' down slowly to the ground. Encourage them to take their time as they listen and move to the music.

6. Next, the children can stand up and repeat the activity with both fingers fluttering and hands floating, taking a long time to reach the floor.

7. Encourage the children to imagine what would happen if the wind caught the leaf as it fell. How would their movements change? Add twirling and spinning.

Games:

▶ Ask the children to make different leaf shapes with their hands and bodies – long, thin, round, pointy, spikey, curly, and so on.

▶ Play any of the music from the 'Songs and music' section below and ask the children to dance around the room, taking care not to bump into anybody.

▶ Ask them to stop when the music stops, ask them to stand still and make a leaf shape.

Songs and music:

'Five Little Leaves so Bright and Gay'
Antonio Vivaldi 'Autumn', (from 'The Four Seasons')
Joseph Kosma 'Autumn Leaves' (jazz standard)
Arthur Bliss 'Approach of Autumn'
Missing Human 'A Cup of Coffee in a Cloudy Afternoon'
Earth, Wind & Fire 'September'
The Moody Blues 'Forever Autumn'
Frank Sinatra 'September Song'
Neil Young 'Harvest Moon'
Ella & Louis 'Autumn in New York'

Taking it further

▶ Use felt leaves attached to ribbons or silk scarves and invite the children to move around the room, weaving in and out of each other and making the leaves flutter, float, fly and fall as they go.

▶ Try some leaf rubbing using thin paper and wax crayons, or leaf printing using autumn-coloured paints and rollers.

Body bending

Related themes: Bodies, All about me, Puppets

What you need:

▶ Recorded music or access to YouTube – see 'Songs and music'
▶ A pair of claves for each child
▶ Hand drum or tambour drum

What you do:

Music makers

▶ Sing 'Heads, Shoulders, Knees and Toes'. Add the actions. Try missing out different words and just performing the actions.

▶ Provide the children with a pair of claves each. Explore different ways of playing the claves: tapping together in the usual way, lengthways, tips together, tapping the floor, and so on.

▶ Choose a piece of music from 'Songs and music' and ask the children to add their claves to the beat.

Moving to music

1. Ask the children to stand in a circle and travel around the room in response to the beat of the hand drum. Steady beat: marching, walking, strolling, etc. Faster beat: running, on tiptoes, forwards and backwards, crawling, etc. Slower beat: jumping, creeping, hopping, etc. Dotted rhythm: skipping, dancing, spinning, galloping, etc.

2. Play 'Fossils' from 'The Carnival of the Animals', or 'Dem Bones'. Ask the children to try moving in different ways in response to the music to create a 'skeleton dance'.

3. Add some of the claves sounds practised in 'Music makers'.

4. Show the children a string puppet. Talk about how it moves. The strings are pulled or released and the limbs of the puppets are either stretched taut or bent and floppy.

5. Ask the children to work with a partner. The children should take turns to be the puppet and the master. Can the puppet make their limbs really floppy and bendy until the master makes them move?

6. Play the song 'Puppet on a String'. Encourage the children to move as puppet and master in response to the song.

7. Play 'Step in Time'. Listen to the different actions listed in the song. Help the children to follow the words and move in time to the song.

Games:

▶ Choose any music from 'Songs and music' and play some traditional music games such as 'Musical bumps', 'Musical statues' and 'Musical chairs'.

Songs and music:

'Heads, Shoulders, Knees and Toes'

'One Finger, One Thumb, Keep Moving'

'If You're Happy And You Know It'

'Knees up, Mother Brown'

Traditional 'Dem Bones'

Sergei Prokofiev 'Dance of the Knights'

Gypsy Kings 'Bamboleo'

Johann Strauss 'Radetzky March'

Sandie Shaw 'Puppet on a String'

Camille Saint-Saëns 'The Carnival of the Animals: Fossils'

Camille Saint-Saëns 'Danse Macabre'

'Step in Time' (from 'Mary Poppins')

Taking it further

▶ Try some finger, hand and feet-printing activities.

▶ Make skeletons using art straws, cotton buds, scissors and glue, mounted on black sugar paper.

▶ Take photographs of the children. Mount on cardboard. Let them cut the picture into four, five or six pieces and then reconstruct them like a jigsaw. Can they complete each other's jigsaw portraits?

Buildings boogie

Related themes: Buildings, Homes, All about me, People who help us

What you need:

▶ Recorded music or access to YouTube – see 'Songs and music'
▶ Pairs of wooden bricks
▶ A selection of musical instruments
▶ Climbing equipment

What you do:

Music makers

▶ Provide each child with a pair of wooden bricks to tap together.
Ask them to tap bricks in time to the beat and sing this song to the
tune of 'London's Burning':

Build a tower,	*x2*
Build it higher,	*x2*
How high?	*x2*
Knock it down, now.	*x2*

▶ Talk about sounds of building site: hammering, sawing, sanding, cranes,
diggers, cement mixers, forklift trucks, and so on. Let the children choose
instruments to make sound effects.

Moving to music

1. Set up an obstacle course using lots of climbing equipment in the design of a
fantasy building – climbing frame, balance beam, tunnel, A-frame, slide, and
so on.

2. Play any of the songs from 'Songs and music' for the children to move to as they go round the obstacle course.

3. Talk about the different workers on a building site and how they might move – builders, carpenters, truck and crane drivers, etc.

4. Let the children mime some of the actions. Start with chopping down trees, sawing planks, sanding wood, hammering wood together, brick laying, driving, etc.

5. Play 'Music for Pieces of Wood'. Ask the children to act out the different actions in response to the music.

6. Play 'Our House' or 'Sixteen Tons'. Help the children to create a coordinated sequence of building actions to move in time to the music.

Games:

▶ Try a 'Building a wall' team game. Use cereal boxes, stuffed with newspaper and wrapped in sugar paper. Place a pile of boxes at one end of the room.

▶ Ask the children to take turns to pick up a brick box, run to the other end of the room and place it on a chalk drawn base. Which team can build the wall using ten bricks quickest?

Songs and music:

Peter Hammers 'I'm going to Build a little House with One Hammer'
Steve Reich 'Music for Pieces of Wood'
Madness 'Our House'
Shakin' Stevens 'This Ole House'
Tennessee Ernie Ford 'Sixteen Tons'
Simon and Garfunkel 'Feelin' Groovy'
Heatwave 'Boogie Nights'
Barde 'Traditional Medieval Music'

Taking it further

▶ Go outside and ask the children to try some 'water painting' on the building walls. What happens when the sun shines on their artwork?

▶ Work together in a small group to create a huge junk castle. Cover different-sized and shaped boxes with paper or paint, add yellow squares for windows, and construct into a castle with towers, turrets, different levels, etc.

Busy birds

Related themes: Birds, Spring, Flight

What you need:

▶ Recorded music or access to YouTube – see 'Songs and music'

▶ A set of chiffon or silk scarves

I will need

What you do:

Music makers

▶ Try some echo singing using the two cuckoo notes, G and E, and the words 'soh' and 'me'. Introduce the Kodály hand signs for these two notes. 'Soh' is the higher note so place your hand in front of your face, palm facing you. 'Me' is the lower note so place your hand lower down, palm facing the floor. Ask the children to copy by singing the notes and making the hand signs.

▶ Use two chime bars or hand chimes, G and E, as the cuckoo call notes. Play patterns using the two notes for the children to echo sing or play.

▶ Listen to 'Le Coucou' by Daquin. Can the children use their hands to show each cuckoo call?

Moving to music

1. Ask the children to find a space in the room where they can stretch their arms out wide without touching anybody else.

2. Ask the children to pretend they are newly hatched chicks in a nest, waiting for their first flying lesson. Can they curl up small like tiny birds? Ask them to slowly uncurl and pop their heads up over the side of the nest. Can they stand up like wobbly baby birds and take a few tentative steps?

3. Play the opening of 'Le Merle Noir' ('The Blackbird') and ask the children to move like the baby bird learning to fly.

4. Talk about the different ways birds move – they might fly, hover, flap, soar, flutter, swoop, dart; or walk, strut, peck, hop, float, waddle, and so on. Give the children opportunity to try out each of these moves.

5. Listen to extracts from 'The Swan' or 'The Aviary' (see 'Songs and music'). Talk to the children about the different ways they could move as birds to this music – floating, gliding, flying, etc. Let them experiment with movements in response to the music.

6. Try some movement with scarves. Scrunch the scarf into a ball and throw it into the air. Watch it unfold, float, and twirl to the ground. Shake the scarf out and practise moving around with it floating at different levels, high and low. Can the children copy these movements with their bodies?

7. Now try moving to the music again, with the scarves. Does using the scarves make it easier to move like birds?

Games:

▶ Play 'Busy Birds' - a game in the style of 'Beans'. Start with two contrasting birds such as 'duck' (waddle – toddle around on two legs) and 'kestrel' (hover in one place with 'wings' outstretched).

▶ Introduce more birds as the children get more confident. Try 'seagull' (loud cries and try to (gently!) peck others), 'swan' (glide around serenely), 'woodpecker' (clap a rhythm as the bird pecks a tree), 'sparrow' (bounce around on two legs), 'owl' (tu-whit-tu-whoo), and so on.

Songs and music:

'Two Little Dickie Birds'

'Five Little Ducks'

Camille Saint-Saëns 'The Carnival of the Animals: The Aviary'

Camille Saint-Saëns 'The Carnival of the Animals: The Swan'

Louis-Claude Daquin 'Le Coucou' ('The Cuckoo')

Olivier Messiaen 'Le Merle Noir' ('The Blackbird') or 'Oiseaux Exotiques' ('Exotic Birds')

Maurice Ravel 'Oiseaux Tristes' ('Sad Birds')

Antonio Vivaldi 'Il Gardellino' ('The Goldfinch')
The Beatles 'Blackbird'
The Tweets 'The Birdie Song'
Kay Kyser 'Woody Woodpecker'
Bobby Day 'Rockin' Robin'

Taking it further

▶ Listen to 'Oiseaux Exotiques' and compare with some real birdsong recordings.
▶ Watch a clip of geese flying in formation. Try some formation dancing! Arrange the children in a large 'V' shape in the room. Can they move together around the room and keep the shape?

Chattering children

Related themes: All about me, Ourselves, Children, Families, Toys, Puppets

What you need:

▶ Recorded music or access to YouTube – see 'Songs and music'

▶ A selection of musical instruments including some tuned percussion

What you do:

Music makers

▶ Sing some gentle lullabies (see 'Songs and music'). Talk about what makes an effective lullaby – gentle rocking rhythm, quiet, and a slow tempo.

▶ Play the children a slow, lilting, repeated pattern using two consecutive notes on a xylophone or metallophone. Allow the children to take turns playing this sleepy pattern.

▶ Provide an instrument for each child in the group. Ask them to show you the quietest sound they can make. Can they play their quiet sounds at the same time as the sleepy pattern?

Moving to music

1. Talk about different types of toys. Ask the children to imagine how each toy might move – toy soldier, teddy bear, rag doll, Barbie doll, tricycle, ball, spinning top, and so on. Can they reproduce the movements with their bodies?

2. Play 'March of the Toy Soldiers'. Invite the children to march around, with stiff arms and legs like toy soldiers.

3. Play 'Rag Doll'. Can the children move around the room like a doll and, when the words 'rag doll' occur, make their bodies as floppy as possible?

4. Play 'La Toupie'. Can the children spin carefully around like a spinning top? Take care not to get too dizzy by changing direction!

5. Play 'Perpetuum Mobile'. Choose a new toy to move with each different instrument section. Use as many of the children's own ideas for movement as possible.

6. On the loud cymbal crash near the end, all the toys must stop moving and gradually unwind and slow down before coming to a stop.

Games:

▶ Play the Toy Story theme, 'You've Got a Friend in Me'. Ask the children to dance as the music plays. When the music stops, ask them to freeze in the shape of one of the toys.

▶ Alternatively, call out a character when the music stops and the children should move appropriately. For example: Buzz Lightyear – pretend to fly like a spaceman; Woody – throw a lasso; Jessie – gallop around; Rex – walk slowly with hands up and two fingers like T-Rex claws; Slinky Dog – walk on all fours, stretched out long and thin; Aliens – get into groups of three, point up and say 'the claw', and so on.

Songs and music:

'Hush, Little Baby'
'Rock-a-Bye Baby'
'Ten in a Bed'
'Boys and Girls Come Out To Play'
'Miss Polly had a Dolly'
Frédérick Chopin 'Berceuse Op.57'
Johannes Brahms 'Lullaby'
Frankie Vallli and the Four Seasons 'Rag Doll'
Claude Debussy 'Serenade for the Doll'
Georges Bizet 'Jeux d'Enfants: Trumpet and Drum'
Georges Bizet 'La Toupie' ('Spinning Top')
Leopold Mozart/Joseph Haydn 'Toy Symphony'
Pyotr Ilyich Tchaikovsky 'March of the Toy Soldiers' (from 'The Nutcracker')
Johann Strauss 'Perpetuum Mobile'
Randy Newman 'You've Got a Friend in Me' (from 'Toy Story')

Taking it further

▶ Act out the song 'Ten in the Bed'. Invite ten children to lie down on a mat or duvet. Sing the song and let them take turns to roll over and pretend to fall out.

▶ Make some finger puppets. Use a basic finger shape and let the children add faces, hats, wings, ears and beaks to create their own special character.

Chinatown

Related themes: China, Chinese New Year, Pitch

What you need:

▶ Recorded music or access to YouTube – see 'Songs and music'
▶ A selection of tuned percussion instruments
▶ Long scarves

What you do:

Music makers

▶ Set up pentatonic scales (five notes – C, D, E, G, A) on tuned percussion instruments. Show the children how to hold the beaters between thumb and forefinger so that the sticks are loose and can bounce on the bars and make the best sound.

▶ Let the children experiment playing the five notes in any order. Listen to the children playing individually. This scale is the basis of a lot of Chinese music.

▶ What happens when the children all play quietly at the same time? It should still sound effective, as the scales interlock with each other.

Moving to music

1. Practise moving at different levels. Ask the children to listen to the pentatonic scale being played very slowly from low to high. Can they move their bodies from low to high with the music?

2. Now try moving from high to low. Show the children how to hold their hands above their heads with their palms pressed together as they sink down.

3. Line up the children and ask them all to slowly move their hands up and down, pressing their palms together at the top and bottom of the movement. Encourage them to move one after the other rather than all at the same time.

4. Then ask every other child to move to the right or left alternately, out of the line, using long sweeping steps, to form three lines in total.

5. Ask the children to stand facing a partner. Provide each pair with long scarves or ribbons. Encourage them to practise holding both ends; one of the children in each pair then lets go and the child holding the scarf/ribbon makes big circles, waves and spirals with the fabric. Join together again and repeat so both the children in each pair get a turn.

6. Play some traditional Chinese music (see 'Songs and music') and ask the children to make slow, graceful movements to fit the sounds.

Games:

▶ Play 'Chinese Dragon's Tail'. Ask the children to stand in a long line with their hands on each other's shoulders. The front child is the dragon's head and the last child is the tail.

▶ The leader (the head) must move around the room, trying to 'tag' the tail without losing any of the middle children or letting the line break. The children in between must do their best to stop the head from catching the tail.

▶ When the head catches the tail, the tail becomes the new head and all the children move down one place.

Songs and music:

'My Ship Sailed from China'
Traditional 'Spring Blossoms on a Moonlit River'
Traditional 'Music for Chinese Instruments' (the Pipa or Guzheng, played by Liu Fang)
Pyotr Ilyich Tchaikovsky 'Chinese Dance' (from 'The Nutcracker')
Tan Dun 'Crouching Tiger, Hidden Dragon' soundtrack

Taking it further

▶ Talk about Chinese New Year. Tell the children the traditional story of the Chinese Zodiac and how the animals took part in a race to show off to the Emperor, ending with the animals giving their names to the different years. Ask the children to act out the story. How will the different animals move?

▶ Try some Chinese paper cutting. Provide the children with a piece of red cardboard, a piece of white or black paper and a pair of scissors. Show them how to fold the white paper and cut shapes out to form pictures and patterns. Mount the finished paper on top of the red card and display.

Circus skills

Related themes: Circus, Celebrations, All about me

What you need:

► Recorded music or access to YouTube – see 'Songs and music'
► Bean bags, skipping ropes, plastic stilts, hula hoops
► Face paints, mirrors, paints and brushes

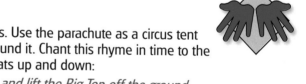

What you do:

Music makers

► Try some parachute games. Use the parachute as a circus tent and let the children sit around it. Chant this rhyme in time to the beat, as the parachute floats up and down:

> *Everybody sit around, and lift the Big Top off the ground.*
> *Up and down, see it grow, the circus tent is ready for the show.*
> *Everybody sit around, and lift the Big Top off the ground.*
> *Horses, jugglers, acrobats, clowns all wearing funny hats.*
> *Everybody sit around, and lift the Big Top off the ground.*
> *Tightrope walkers balancing, the Master paces round the ring.*
> *Everybody sit around, and lift the Big Top off the ground.*
> *Now the show is almost done, and we've all had circus fun.*

Moving to music

1. Try using some small equipment to develop control and coordination skills. Provide each child with a coloured bean bag. Can they move around while balancing the bean bag on one hand, their heads or their backs?

2. Try some simple juggling moves. Throw the beanbag up into the air and catch it with two hands. Then try catching it with one hand.

3. Play 'Yakety Sax'. How fast can the children move around or juggle with their bean bag without dropping it?

4. Talk about different circus skills. Ask the children to share any experiences of visiting the circus. Watch film clips of juggling, acrobats and clowns.

5. Set up four different circus stations: clowns, juggling, tightrope walking and stilt walking.

6. Let the children try out these moves. Clowns – pulling faces, doing handstands, cartwheels, etc. Juggling – use juggling balls or bean bags. Tightrope walker – stretch a skipping rope on the floor for the children to balance on. Stilt walking – practise walking on plastic stilts.

6. Play 'Entry of the Gladiators'. Let the children perform their skills in the groups as the music plays.

Games:

▶ Play a game of 'The Ringmaster says' based on the traditional game 'Simon Says'. The children must only obey the command if it is prefaced with the phrase 'The Ringmaster says'. Make the actions circus-related: 'dance like clowns', 'touch your toes', 'walk the tightrope', 'jump in the air' etc.

Songs and music:

Antonín Dvořák 'Slavonic Dance No. 8'
Aaron Copland 'Dream March and Circus Music'
Julius Fucik 'Entry of the Gladiators'
Smokey Robinson 'The Tears of a Clown'
Manfred Mann 'Ha! Ha! Said the Clown'
James Rich 'Yakety Sax'
Erik Satie 'Gymnopédie No.1'
John Philip Sousa 'The Liberty Bell'

Taking it further

▶ Ask the children to find a partner. Can they sit facing their partner holding a hoop and rowing back and forwards? Who can hula hoop for the longest? Can they make up some other tricks using the hoops?

▶ Use face paints to make up the children's face like clowns. Provide hand mirrors and ask them to paint clown self-portraits.

Dinosaurs dancing

Related themes: Dinosaurs, Opposites

What you need:

▶ Recorded music or access to YouTube – see 'Songs and music'
▶ Drums, tambours or tambourines

What you do:

Music makers

▶ Sing this song to the tune of 'The Grand old Duke of York':

Oh the great big dinosaur,
He moved along the ground,
He swung his tail and stretched his neck,
And he didn't make a sound.

▶ Add the beat or pulse on soft drums or tambours.

Moving to music

1. Ask the children to move around the room as some of the children sing and play the dinosaur song from 'Music makers'. Can they move slowly in time to the beat?

2. Move about like a big, strong Brachiosaurus. Use heavy, long strides and move slowly around the area. Try using one hand as a swinging tail and the other as the dinosaur's neck, stretching up to pick leaves from trees.

3. Change to the small, fast-moving Velociraptor. Run on tiptoes, in and out of trees, looking around all the time.

4. Play 'I Believe I Can Fly'. Stretch hands wide like wings and try gliding, soaring high and low like a Pterosaur.

5. Crawl around on all fours, slowly and stiffly, like a bony-plated Stegosaurus.

6. Ask the children to find a space and curl up as small as they can. Now they are the dinosaur egg and the whole adventure can begin!

7. Play the 'Jurassic Park' theme tune. Ask the children to start as a dinosaur egg and then hatch and move like different dinosaurs as the music changes.

Games:

▶ Play 'Fossils' from 'The Carnival of the Animals'. Invite the children to move around like the dinosaur of their choice until the music stops. Then they must freeze in a dinosaur shape. Anybody still moving is out.

▶ Make it harder by changing the surface the dinosaurs are moving on – in and out of puddles, through a slimy swamp, on spikey gravel, through thick undergrowth, trying not to be seen by bigger dinosaurs!

Songs and music:

Johnny Cash 'The Dinosaur Song'
Was Not Was 'Walk the Dinosaur'
Benjamin Bartlett 'Walking with Dinosaurs'
R. Kelly 'I Believe I Can Fly'
John Williams 'Jurassic Park Theme'
Camille Saint-Saëns 'The Carnival of the Animals: Fossils'

Taking it further

▶ Ask the children to stand in a long line and move around following the leader. Play 'Walk the Dinosaur' as they move around the room. Make up some crazy dinosaur dance moves.

▶ Make some junk dinosaurs from egg boxes, cardboard boxes, tubes, tea bag cartons, art straws, buttons and other materials.

Elegant elephants

Related themes: Elephants, Animals, Pitch

What you need:

▶ Recorded music or access to YouTube – see 'Songs and music'
▶ A selection of tuned percussion instruments such as boomwhackers, hand chimes, xylophones or metallophones

What you do:

Music makers

▶ Talk about 'pitch' (high and low sounds) to the children and explain that big instruments play low sounds while small instruments play high sounds. Relate to voices – dad has a low voice, children have high voices.

▶ Demonstrate with instruments; boomwhackers and hand chimes are good visual aids. Choose a low sounding note and contrast it with a high note. Ask the children to stand up when they hear the high sound and sit down when they hear the low sound.

▶ Let the children take turns playing the high and low sounds for the others to move to.

Moving to music

1. Play 'The Elephant'. This solo was written for the biggest and lowest string instrument in the orchestra, the double bass. Talk about why this is a good choice to represent the elephant.

2. Try out some elephant moves – plodding along with slow, giant steps; swaying slowly from side to side; swinging one arm as a trunk; picking leaves from the trees with the 'trunk' arm; sucking up and squirting water with the trunk; and so on.

3. Watch some footage of elephants moving on YouTube. Does this add to the repertoire of moves the children can think of?

4. Stand in a circle and invite the children to move around like elephants, using all of their ideas for moves.

5. Put together a sequence of moves for the children to make as they listen to 'The Elephant'.

6. Play 'Baby Elephant Walk'. Will their elephant moves change to this different style of music?

Games:

▶ Use the song 'One Grey Elephant Balancing' and invite the children to act it out by balancing on a stretched-out skipping rope. How many elephants can they get to balance together?

▶ Alternatively, draw a giant spider's web on the playground using chalk and try the other rhyme 'One Elephant Went Out to Play'.

Songs and music:

'I Went to the Animal Fair'
'An Elephant Walks Like This and That'
'One Elephant Went out to Play'
'One Grey Elephant Balancing'
Mandy Miller 'Nellie the Elephant'
Oliver Wallace 'When I See An Elephant Fly' (from 'Dumbo')
Tom Paxton 'Daddy's Taking Us To The Zoo Tomorrow'
Henry Mancini 'Baby Elephant Walk'
Camille Saint-Saëns 'The Carnival of the Animals: The Elephant'
Francis Poulenc 'L'Histoire de Babar, Le Petit Éléphant'

Taking it further

▶ Watch online clips of elephants making music: listen to the Thai Elephant Orchestra or an elephant playing the piano!

▶ Make an Elmer elephant from a recycled plastic 4-pint milk bottle. Cut across the middle of the handle and bottle. Cut an arch in each of the four sides for the legs and leave the handle as the trunk. Cut across the top just under the lid to flatten the back and stick a piece of card over the whole. Cover in watered-down PVA glue and stick patchwork coloured squares all over!

Farmyard frolics

Related themes: Farms, Animals

What you need:

▶ Recorded music or access to YouTube – see 'Songs and music'
▶ A selection of different musical instruments

What you do:

Music makers

▶ Sing 'Old MacDonald' or 'I Went To Visit The Farm' and encourage the children to make farm animal noises with their voices.

▶ Can they choose an instrument to go with each animal? Does the guiro sound like a pig grunting? Do the castanets sound like a horse clip-clopping along?

Moving to music

1. Make a list of different farm animals – sheep, horses, cows, hens, pigs, and so on. Talk about the ways the animals might move.

2. Play 'The Happy Farmer'. Ask the children to choose an animal and find a space in the room as the music plays. Let them get into a starting position.

3. Then use the different musical examples (see 'Songs and music') to inspire the children to move in imaginative ways as different animals. Just use small excerpts from each piece.

4. Play 'Horn Concerto' and invite the children to gallop around the room like horses.

5. Play 'Sheep May Safely Graze' and ask the children to move slowly around while munching the grass.

6. Play 'Hens and Cockerels' from 'The Carnival of the Animals'. Can the children move around the room, pecking for corn like hens?

7. Play 'Cincinatti Dancing Pig' and let the children finish by being pigs rolling in mud and tap-dancing a jig!

Games:

▶ Play the traditional game 'The Farmer's in his Den'.

▶ Sit in a circle and play 'Duck, duck, goose' or change the animals to 'Pig, pig, piglet' or 'Cow, cow, bull'.

Songs and music:

'Old MacDonald Had A Farm'
'I Went to Visit the Farm One Day'
'Baa Baa Black Sheep'
'One Man Went To Mow'
'The Farmer's in his Den'
J.S. Bach 'Sheep May Safely Graze'
Camille Saint-Saëns 'The Carnival of the Animals: Hens and Cockerels'
Wolfgang Amadeus Mozart 'Horn Concerto No.4 Rondo'
Red Foley 'Cincinnati Dancing Pig'
Jacques Offenbach 'Infernal Galop'
Robert Schumann 'The Happy Farmer'
Aaron Copland 'I Bought Me a Cat'
Jayla 'Waddle We Do'

Taking it further

▶ Try a 'Duck waddle race'. Ask the children to squat down at the starting line and grasp their ankles from behind. Can they waddle as fast as possible to the finishing line? Play 'Waddle We Do' as the children race.

▶ Ask the children to work in a group to make a farm collage. Divide a large piece of cardboard into six squares. Use a variety of materials to create each field such as corrugated card, felt, fake grass, yellow netting and shiny blue paper. Let the children play on the farm board using small play farm animals.

Festivals of food

Related themes: Food, Celebrations

What you need:

▶ Recorded music or access to YouTube – see 'Songs and music'
▶ A variety of instruments to shake - maracas, rattles, bells, tambourines

What you do:

Music makers

▶ Sing the song 'Jelly on the Plate'. Ask the children to choose instruments to play while singing the 'wibble wobble' line.
▶ Change the musical sounds to match different types of food such as 'biscuits in the tin' or 'sausages in the pan'.

Moving to music

1. Ask the children to find a space. Can they wobble one arm at a time? Now try wobbling both legs. Add a wobbly head. Can they walk around the room like a jelly?
2. Play some music from 'Music makers' for the children to move in response.
3. Blow some bubbles into the air and invite small groups of the children to try and pop them. Tell them they can use one finger only. Encourage them to jump up high to catch all the bubbles.
4. Invite the children to make bubble shapes with their arms and ask a partner to 'pop' the imaginary bubbles.

5. Play the song 'Popcorn'. Invite the children to find a space. Can they imagine they are the popcorn in a pan? Stand on the spot, extending arms and legs, and pointing fingers and toes in time to the beat of the music.

6. Divide the children into small circles of six, with the children in each circle holding hands. Ask the circles to move around the room during the high string part of 'Popcorn' (1:08 minutes in).

7. They should return to making popping moves when the popping sounds return and fade to a stand still.

8. Watch the music video to 'Hot Potato'. Can the children join in the words and the dance moves? Make up some new foodie words and moves of your own.

Games:

▶ Play the game 'Fruit salad'. All the children sit on chairs arranged in a circle. Give each child the name of a fruit, either 'apple', 'orange' or 'banana'.

▶ When you call out each fruit, those with that name must stand up and change seats.

▶ On the call 'fruit salad', all the children must change seats.

▶ When the children are familiar with the game, try removing chairs so that the last to find a seat are 'out'.

Songs and music:

'Pease Pudding Hot'
'Five Currant Buns'
'Five Fat Sausages'
'One Potato'
'Jelly on the Plate'
'Hot Cross Buns'
Hot Butter 'Popcorn'
Lionel Bart 'Food, Glorious Food' (from 'Oliver!')
Cab Calloway 'Everybody Eats When They Come To My House'
Hans Christian Lumbye 'Champagne Galop'
Sesame Street 'Healthy Food'
The Wiggles 'Hot Potato'

Taking it further

▶ Play 'Everybody Eats When They Come To My House'. Listen to the words of the song carefully. Can any children find food that rhymes with their name?

▶ Make some popcorn for the children to share together at snack time. Let them look at the corn before it is cooked, and listen to the corn popping as it cooks in the saucepan or microwave.

Fireworks display

Related themes: Fireworks, Autumn, Celebrations, Stars

What you need:

- ▶ Recorded music or access to YouTube – see 'Songs and music'
- ▶ Short sticks with loops or bunches of tinsel attached to make 'firework sticks'
- ▶ A selection of musical instruments – maracas, cabasas, tambourine, drum, swannee whistle, castanets, etc.

What you do:

Music makers

- ▶ Talk about the sounds of fireworks – bang, crash, squeal, fizz, pop, crackle, etc.
- ▶ Listen to some sound effects on YouTube. Can the children make some of the sounds using their voices? Encourage them to practise!
- ▶ Sort the children into groups of different firework sounds. Point at the groups in turn to make their sounds in a sequence. Let the children take turns to conduct the 'firework display' and don't forget to applaud at the end!
- ▶ Provide a selection of musical instruments and ask the children to explore different firework sounds. Does the maraca sound like a 'sparkler' or the tambourine like a 'rocket'? Make another 'firework display' using the instruments.

Moving to music

1. Play 'La Rejouissance' and ask the children what they think the music is describing. Watch a film of fireworks being set off while this piece of music

plays on YouTube. Can they hear how the fireworks try to coincide with the loud cymbals and drums?

2. Ask the children to find a space to stand.

3. Sing 'Twinkle, Twinkle, Little Star' and add actions: open and close hands into a star shape, and make a diamond with index fingers and thumbs in the middle of the song.

4. Play the music again and invite the children to make a star or firework shape with their hands; they fling their hands into the sky each time they hear the cymbals.

5. Can they make firework shapes with their whole bodies? Encourage them to try star jumps or tuck jumps.

6. Ask the children to move around on tiptoe, taking care not to bump into anybody as the music plays. Can they coincide their star shapes with the loud sounds in the music? Remind them to use their bodies not their voices!

Games:
▶ Provide the children with 'firework sticks' and show them how to move these in circles and spirals, like sparks from a firework.

▶ Play any of the music from the 'Songs and music' section below and invite the children to stand on the spot and move the sticks around in the air.

▶ When the music stops can they make their firework stick move very slowly to the ground as the firework goes out.

Songs and music:

'Twinkle, Twinkle, Little Star'
Oliver Knussen 'Flourish with Fireworks'
Igor Stravinsky 'Feu d'artifice'
Claude Debussy 'Feux d'artifice'
George Frideric Handel 'La Réjouissance' (from 'Music for the Royal Fireworks')
Katy Perry 'Firework'

Taking it further
▶ Ask the children to crouch down on the floor and make themselves as small as possible. Count down from ten to zero together; on zero, the children can jump into the air as high as they can, like a firework rocket.

▶ Try some painting to music. Choose some music from 'Songs and music', above, and provide the children with large piece of black sugar paper on an easel and lots of brightly-coloured or florescent paints.

Floating in space

Related themes: Space, Night and Day, Stars, Pitch

What you need:

▶ Recorded music or access to YouTube – see 'Songs and music'
▶ Bubble mixture and a variety of bubble blowers

What you do:

Music makers

▶ Play 'Silent bubbles'. Draw a row of four circles or 'bubbles' on the white board. Choose two words about space, one with one syllable and one with two, such as 'space' and 'rocket', and write one of them inside each bubble, e.g. 'space', 'space, (silence), 'rocket', 'rocket'.

▶ Practise saying and clapping the rhythm of the words. Then invite a child to come and 'pop' one of the bubbles by rubbing out the word. Say and clap the words again and leave a silence or 'rest' in the gap – 'space', 'space, (silence), 'rocket', 'rocket'.

▶ Continue until there are four silences!

▶ To increase the difficulty, next round choose words with more syllables and draw another row of four bubbles on the board.

Moving to music

1. Ask the children to find a space to stand in the room.

2. Explain that, because of zero gravity, everything appears to move in slow motion in space. Have fun trying to move in slow motion. Can they control their arms and legs as they pretend to walk or run? Can they reach out to the side or up high very slowly? What happens if they fall in slow motion?

3. Play 'Chariots of Fire'. Let the children move in slow motion to the music.

4. Focus on walking very slowly using giant steps around the room. This is probably what it would be like to walk on the surface of the moon.

5. Play 'Walking on the Moon'. Invite the children to walk around during the opening chords, taking giant strides, and freezing when the music stops.

6. Now combine this with floating in space, play 'Under Stars' or 'Atmospheres' and ask the children to imagine that they are wearing a space suit and are floating through space, moving slowly, supported by the space around them.

Games:

▶ Ask the children to crouch down low and then count down from 10 - 0 together. On zero they must move slowly up into the air like rockets taking off. Who can reach the highest?

▶ Can they use their voices from low to high as they move their bodies?

▶ Reverse it and try a rocket landing with the bodies and voices moving from high to low.

▶ Let the children take turns to blow bubbles into the space for the rockets to touch.

Songs and music:

Vangelis 'Chariots of Fire'
Richard Strauss 'Also Sprach Zarathustra'
Holst 'The Planets Suite'
David Bowie 'Space Oddity'
Sesame Street 'I Dont Want to Live on the Moon'
Kraftwerk 'Spacelab'
Frank Sinatra 'Fly me to the Moon'
The Police 'Walking on the Moon'
John Williams 'Cantina Song' (from 'Star Wars')
Brian Eno 'Under Stars'
Ligeti 'Atmospheres'

Taking it further

▶ Make up an alien dance to 'Cantina Song' from 'Star Wars'.

▶ Try some bubble painting. Mix a small amount of bubble mixture into some runny paint. Pour it into empty ice cream pots and blow with a straw until lots of bubbles foam up. Place a piece of paper on top of the bubbles.

Growing grooves

Related themes: Growth, Spring, Children, All about me, Families

What you need:

▶ Recorded music or access to YouTube – see 'Songs and music'
▶ A selection of tuned percussion instruments
▶ Colourful packets of seeds

I will need

What you do:

Music makers

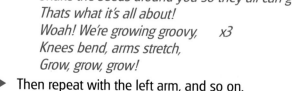

▶ Provide the children with seed packets to shake (it's a good idea to cover the packets with clear sticky plastic to preserve them). Try out different packets to find the best shakers!

▶ Ask the children to stand in a circle and shake the seeds as they sing this song to the tune of 'The Hokey Cokey':

You put your right arm in,
Your right arm out,
In, out, in, out, shake them all about.
Shake the seeds around you so they all can grow,
Thats what it's all about!
Woah! We're growing groovy,   x3
Knees bend, arms stretch,
Grow, grow, grow!

▶ Then repeat with the left arm, and so on.

Moving to music

1. Practise moving at different levels. Ask the children to listen to a musical scale being played very slowly from low to high. Can they move their bodies from low to high with the music? Then reverse – move from high to low.

2. Play the lowest note followed by the highest note. Can the children jump up as high as they can each time they hear the music jump up?

3. Play 'Jumping Bean'. Invite the children to take turns to demonstrate their jumping skills in response to this music. Can they jump up, sideways, forwards, backwards? Try some fancy star jumps, tuck jumps, split leaps, and so on. Organise the jumps into a simple sequence.

4. Play 'The Hippy Hippy Shake'. Ask the children to stand in a space. Start by shaking their hands, then feet, then arms and legs, and move onto head and bottom.

Games:

▶ Play 'Grandmother's Footsteps'. Who can creep up and surprise Grandma?

▶ Play 'Greetings, Your Majesty'. One child is chosen to be the king or queen and sits on a chair facing the wall. Invite the other children to take turns to be the royal visitor and greet the king or queen, who has his/her back to the visitor. Can the children recognise each other's voices?

Songs and music:

'One Finger, One Thumb'
'If You're Happy And You Know It'
Robert Farnon 'Jumping Bean'
The Beatles 'The Hippy Hippy Shake'
The Beatles 'Twist and Shout'

Taking it further

▶ Ask the children to create a self-portrait. Provide hand mirrors so they can look closely at their faces. Let them use paints or collage materials.

▶ Try a yoga flower pose: ask the children to sit on the floor and press the soles of their feet together. Can they keep their back straight? Move the hands so they are underneath the ankles and lift the feet off the floor while breathing out slowly.

▶ Try a yoga tree pose: ask the children to stand up tall. Hold out the arms to provide balance. Can they move one of their feet off the floor and slide it up the other leg to just below the knee? Move the arms above the head, press hands together and look up. Balance.

Indian images

Related themes: India, Diwali, Animals, All about me

What you need:

▶ Recorded music or access to YouTube – see 'Songs and music'
▶ Tuned percussion instruments
▶ A selection of Indian bells or finger cymbals, wrist and ankle bells

What you do:

Music makers

▶ Introduce the idea of the drone: long, resonating sounds, usually played on the tambura (an Indian string instrument). Play some long sounds on a guitar by plucking the open string G. Or use the open string G on a violin or cello. Or hand chimes C and G together.

▶ Set up a raga (Indian scale) on some tuned percussion. Use the notes C, D, E, F, G, A, B and ask the children to take turns to play any patterns using these notes while you play the drone notes.

Moving to music

1. Watch some Indian dance and talk about the hand gestures or 'hastas'. Teach the children some simple animal hastas such as 'the bee' (single hand) – curl the index finger on top of the thumb, and close the middle finger on the tip of the thumb while extending the other two fingers; and 'the flying bird' (double hand) – with palms facing, link the thumbs together and make the hands undulate like wings.

2. Play some Indian music (see 'Songs and music'). Ask the children to stand still in a space and make the hand gestures. Can they follow their hand movements with their eyes?

3. Learn some more hastas. Try:

▶ 'The deer' – raise the little finger and thumb upwards and bend the other fingers at 90 degrees.

▶ 'The peacock' – hold the hand up high with fingers extended upwards, join the tips of the ring finger and thumb.

▶ 'The snake' – hold the hand high with fingers close together, bend over the tips of the fingers slightly.

▶ 'The fish' – place the right palm over the back of the left hand, fingers together and extend both thumbs out.

4. Invite the children to work with a partner; each child should choose a different animal and they should dance together as they listen to the music. Let the children wear bells on their ankles or wrists, and use finger cymbals to add bell sounds to the dance.

Games:

▶ Play the traditional English game 'Rock, paper, scissors', and talk about the hand gestures involved.

▶ Try a traditional Indian game: 'In the pond, on the bank'. Draw a circle in chalk and ask the children to stand around the circle. When you shout 'In the pond!' they must all jump, feet together, inside the circle. On the command 'On the bank!', they must all jump, feet together, outside the circle.

▶ Add a new move – shout 'Bridge!' and all the children must jump and land with their feet either side of the circle.

Songs and music:

www.mamalisa.com – lots of different children's songs from around the world

Pandit Ravi Shankar 'Raga Rasia'

Ravi Shankar and Philip Glass 'Passages'

Anoushka Shankar 'Raga Desh'

Mohammad Rafi 'Baharon Phool Barsao'

Bollywood songs

Taking it further

▶ Look at images of Mehndi designs painted on hands. This is a traditional art using henna, used for Indian celebrations such as Diwali and weddings. Ask the children to draw around their hand and then help them cut out the shape. Let them draw their own patterns and designs on the handprints.

Minibeasts on the move

Related themes: Minibeasts, Spring, Summer, Animals, Tempo

What you need:

- ▶ Recorded music or access to YouTube – see 'Songs and music'
- ▶ Short lengths of velvet ribbon, each with a loop sewn at one end and pompom or googly eyes
- ▶ Two picture cards of a bumblebee and a snail
- ▶ Collage materials

What you do:

Music makers

- ▶ Let the children choose a velvet 'worm' and thread it onto their index finger. Show them how to make it wriggle in the air and on the floor.
- ▶ Sing this song to the tune of 'Knees up Mother Brown':

   Wriggle like a worm,   x2
   Wriggle, wriggle, wriggle, wriggle,
   Wriggle like a worm.

Moving to music

1. Ask the children to find a space.
2. Tell them to travel around the room on tiptoes, taking care not to bump into anyone. On your signal, they should stop and stretch up to make a long shape in the air. Repeat, but this time when they stop they should make a curled up shape. Repeat once more, stop and make a long shape on the ground.

3. Play 'Music for Snails'. Ask the children to listen to the slow tempo (speed) of the music and move with it like a snail. Can they curl up in their shell? They should stretch out slowly to see what is ahead of them. Curl up again. Stretch out and move slowly along the floor in time to the music.

4. Contrast the slow movement of the snail with the quick darting movements of a fly or a bee. Play 'Flight of the Bumblebee' or 'Diary of a Fly'.

5. Use the picture cards of the bee and the snail as visual cues for the children to change their movements accordingly.

6. Add a spider to the mix and play 'Tarantella Napolitana'. Invite two children to join hands and be the spider. How will the spider move? Can the two the children move together slowly, creeping along, and then pounce?

7. Ask some of the children to join hands in a circle. Invite others to join hands in straight lines across the circle to form the spider's web. Ask one of the children to be a fly. Can the spider move fast enough to catch the fly?

Games:

▶ This game, 'Minibeast mix', is in the style of 'Beans', but the children move in the manner of minibeasts. Choose two contrasting minibeasts to start with, such as a bumblebee (fly around and buzz) and a frog (jump around).

▶ Add more minibeasts to the mix. Try a worm – slither on the ground; spider – find a partner, stand back to back and spin; a fly – dart around, then stop suddenly; a butterfly – flutter gracefully around; a ladybird – mince around on tiptoes; a line of ants – hands above heads, pretending to carry food; a centipede – all the children join together in a long line, holding onto each other's waists.

Songs and music:

'Incy Wincy Spider'
'Little Miss Muffet'
'The Ants Go Marching One By One'
'There Was An Old Lady Who Swallowed A Fly'
'The Ugly Bug Ball'
Nikolai Rimsky-Korsakov 'Flight of the Bumblebee'
Béla Bartok 'Diary of a Fly'
Ralph Vaughan Williams 'Overture to The Wasps'
Josquin des Prez 'El Grillo' ('The Cricket')
Robert Schumann 'Papillons' ('Butterflies')
William Haskell Levine 'Music for Snails'
'Tarantella Napolitana' (from 'The Godfather')
Chet Atkins 'Centipede Boogie'

Taking it further

▶ Collect lots of different movement words that are connected to minibeasts – 'fly', 'scamper', 'crawl', 'hover', 'slither', 'scurry', 'flit', 'flutter', 'creep', 'curl', 'climb', 'spin', 'hop', 'jump', and so on. Ask the children to choose a word and demonstrate it to the group.

▶ Provide lots of different materials such as wooden dolly pegs, pipe cleaners, netting, fabric, beads, tissue paper, paint, etc. for the children to design and construct fantasy minibeasts.

Moving machines

Related themes: Machines, Journeys, Robots

What you need:

▶ Recorded music or access to YouTube – see 'Songs and music'
▶ A collection of musical instruments, including tuned and untuned percussion

What you do:

Music makers

▶ Show the children some machines that make music such as a piano, an electronic keyboard or a drum machine. Talk about how they work.
▶ Watch the music video 'Pipe Dream'.
▶ Make a musical machine by placing a set of instruments in a circle and inviting a group of the children to sit down around the circle, one child behind each instrument. Ask the children to play one sound on each instrument in turn, while moving around the circle. Film with a high definition camcorder and watch back.

Moving to music

1. Talk about lots of different machines: in the home, on the road, on a building site and in factories.
2. Play 'First Construction in Metal'. Invite the children to move like a machine of their choice as they listen.

3. Ask the children to find a space. Invite them to choose a machine movement to copy, such as bending and stretching arms or legs, jumping, punching the air and so on. Can they repeat the movement over and over again?

4. Now ask them to add a machine sound to each movement, using their voices.

5. Ask the children to work with a partner and combine their movements and sounds. Can they make their movements and sounds interact with each other?

6. Make group machines involving four or more children all moving and vocalising together. Walk around the class, 'starting' and 'stopping' the machines. Try speeding up and slowing down the machines. Invite a child to go round and operate the machines.

7. Play 'The Syncopated Clock'. Ask the children to make their group machines move in time to the ticking clock. Can they adjust during the syncopated moments (rhythms that make the music off-beat)?

Games:

▶ Play 'The Robots' and invite the children to move around like robots. Can they make their movements stiff and jerky, as if they are metal machines?

▶ Show the children a remote control and explain that you are going to use it to control their movements.

▶ Ask them to stand up in a space and pretend to be robots. Can they follow all of your controls? Try the controls 'walk', 'forwards', 'backwards', 'bend', 'jump', 'hop', 'jog', 'spin', and so on.

Songs and music:

'Hickory Dickory Dock'
Leroy Anderson 'The Typewriter'
Leroy Anderson 'The Syncopated Clock'
John Cage 'First Construction in Metal'
'Get up off of that thing' (from 'Robots')
Animusic.com 'Pipe Dream'
Kraftwerk 'The Robots'

Taking it further

▶ Use simple machines such as hole punches, staples, and pencil sharpeners to create 3D model machines using strips of paper, card and felt.

▶ Work together and build a giant junk robot. Use cardboard boxes, tubes, egg boxes, aluminum foil trays, plastic lids, metal bottle tops, and so on. Spray with silver or gold paint.

Night and day dreams

Related themes: Night and day, Opposites, Animals

What you need:

▶ Recorded music or access to YouTube – see 'Songs and music'
▶ A selection of musical instruments

What you do:

Music makers

▶ Talk about the difference between night and day sounds. Contrast the quiet calm night with the busy rhythmic day. Help the children to create appropriate soundscapes for the night and day.

▶ Night – gentle long sounds on metallophones, hand chimes, rain sticks, keyboards, interrupted by occasional quiet scratching or scraping on drums, creaking guiros, and ticking clocks. Add nocturnal animal sounds – hooting owls, meowing cats, howling wolves.

▶ Day – repeated rhythms on drums, footsteps walking on the beat, loud traffic sounds using shakers and rattles. Add voices talking, singing, shouting, etc.

Moving to music

1. Talk about different night and day activities. What are the children's favourite daytime activities? Children should take it in turns to mime playing, eating, reading, watching TV, walking, riding a bike, playing football, etc. for others to guess.

2. Choose a sequence of daytime movements to make as the children play the soundscape from 'Music makers'.

3. Repeat the activity with the nighttime activities and sounds. Mime restless sleeping, dreaming, sleep-walking, creeping around in the dark and sudden sounds.

4. Play 'I Got Rhythm'. Show the children how to do a simple 'daytime' dance. Step to one side on the beat and clap hands. Next, step to the other side and replace the clap with a flick kick. Then add alternate straight arms – stretch left arm out as you step left, and vice versa. Mix and match the rhythmic moves.

5. Play 'Five Pieces for Orchestra'. Let the children explore gentle graceful dance moves interjected by sudden stops, jumps and falls in time with the changes in the music.

Games:

▶ Play 'What's the time, Mr Wolf?' Choose one child to stand at one end of the space, turn away from the other children and close his or her eyes. All the other children must chant together: 'What's the time, Mr Wolf?'

▶ If Mr Wolf says '3 o'clock', they can take 3 steps towards him, and so on. If he says 'dinner time', Mr Wolf must turn around and try to catch the children. If he says 'Nighttime', all the children must lie down and pretend to go to sleep.

▶ When a child manages to creep up close enough to touch Mr Wolf, or is caught by Mr Wolf, he takes over.

Songs and music:

'Twinkle, Twinkle, Little Star'
'Star Light, Star Bright'
Johannes Brahms 'Lullaby'
Judith Weir 'Stars, Night, Music and Light'
Anton Webern 'Five Pieces for Orchestra'
Don McLean 'Vincent' ('Starry, Starry Night')
Ludwig van Beethoven 'Moonlight Sonata'
Claude Debussy 'Clair de Lune'

Modest Mussorgsky 'Night on the Bare Mountain'
Disney 'When You Wish Upon a Star' (from 'Pinocchio')
Edvard Grieg 'Morning Mood'
George Gershwin 'I Got Rhythm'
Charles Griffes 'Clouds'
Cole Porter 'Night and Day'

Taking it further

▶ Play 'Clouds'. Invite the children to lie on the ground outside and look up at the clouds as they listen. Can they see any pictures or shapes in the clouds that represent things?

▶ Provide the children with some black sugar paper, white and coloured chalks, sequins and stars, glitter and glue, and ask them to create a collage of the night sky.

Round and round the garden

Related themes: Gardens, Spring, Summer, Growth

What you need:

▶ Recorded music or access to YouTube – see 'Songs and music'
▶ Pairs of small plant pots
▶ Large, colourful flowers made from laminated card

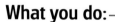

What you do:

Music makers

▶ Sit in a circle and provide each child with a pair of small plant pots. Show them how to tap the bottoms of the pots together.
▶ Ask the children to tap the pots together as they sing this song to the tune of 'In and out the dusky bluebells':

Tap, tap, tap, tap, to the beat,   x 3
Tap to the beat together.
Tap, tap, tap, tap, in the garden, x 3
Whatever the weather.

Moving to music

1. Ask the children to each find a space.

2. As an introduction to the activity, invite them to act out some of the different movements involved in gardening: digging, weeding, mowing, planting seeds, watering the plants, picking flowers, and so on.

3. Ask the children to devise a sequence of moves using their ideas.

4. Once the children are familiar with using their bodies to play out different actions, explain that they are now going to use their bodies to become the seeds and flowers themselves! Play 'Waltz of the Flowers'.

5. During the intro, ask the children to move into a space and curl up very small like a seed. Listen to the harp glissandos. Ask the children to grow up from the ground each time they hear one, blossoming into different flowers in the garden.

6. When the 'waltz' begins, invite individual children to move around the room, in and out of the other children in the garden. Can they hear the '1, 2, 3' count of the music as they move?

7. Remind the children about all the different movements they can make. Try kneeling down and weeding the flowers, or reaching up and using the watering can.

Games:

▶ Place the cardboard flowers on the floor in a random pattern, to represent the garden. Invite the children to each choose one flower to stand on.

▶ Play any of the music from the 'Songs and music' section below, and ask the children to dance around the flowers when the music starts, taking care not to step on any of them.

▶ When the music stops they must quickly find a flower to stand on again.

▶ If preferred, remove a flower each time so the number of children dancing reduces until there is a winner.

Songs and music:

'Mary, Mary, Quite Contrary'

'I Went to the Garden'

'Round and Round the Garden'

Pyotr Ilyich Tchaikovsky 'Waltz of the Flowers' (from 'The Nutcracker')

Claude Debussy 'Estampes: Jardins Sous la Pluie'

Jimmie Rodgers 'English Country Garden'

William Byrd 'All in a Garden Green'

The Beatles 'Octopus's Garden'

Taking it further

▶ Access YouTube and watch the video of 'English Country Garden', sung by Jimmie Rodgers. Draw attention to all the varieties of flowers, insects and birds named in the song, and encourage the children to make some of the different shapes using their bodies.

▶ Go outside and make some sketches of the garden using pencils, pastels and chalks.

▶ Look at some famous paintings of gardens by Claude Monet. Invite the children to bring in photos of their home gardens and use them as a guide for their own paintings.

▶ Design a new garden using simple computer paint software.

Shoe shuffle

Related themes: Shoes, All about me, Clothes

What you need:

► Recorded music or access to YouTube – see 'Songs and music'
► Pairs of wellington boots

What you do:

Music makers

► Ask the children to sit in a circle and each take off one of their shoes.
► Can they tap their shoe on the floor in time to the beat as they sing this song to the tune of 'Rain, Rain, Go Away'?

Feel the beat with your feet,
Feel the beat all down the street.
Feel the beat with your shoe,
Let us see what you can do!

Moving to music

1. Ask the children to find a space in the hall and put on their dancing or PE shoes.

2. Can they travel about the room in different ways in their shoes? Try tiptoes, giant steps, marching, backwards, skipping, stamping, galloping and creeping.

3. Play 'Cinderella Goes To The Ball'. As the music changes, invite the children to move in the different ways they have practised, taking care not to bump into anybody. Can they match fast-moving steps to the faster dance music? How will they move when the music slows down?

4. Watch a fine example of a soft shoe shuffle, danced by Laurel and Hardy in the 1937 film 'Way out West' to the song 'At the Ball'.

5. Invite the children to find a partner and try out some soft shoe shuffle moves.

6. Play 'I Wish' from the film 'Happy Feet'. Can the children try some tap dancing like Mumble the penguin?

Games:

▶ Play this traditional shoe-passing game. Ask each child to take off one shoe again and hold it in their right hand. Can they pass it to the child on their right and tap the floor while chanting the following rhyme?

I will pass this shoe, from me to you, to you,
I will pass this shoe, and do just as I do.

▶ On the last line, the children have to copy any action with the shoe they are holding, such as tapping their knee, shuffling the shoe on the floor, waving the shoe in the air, etc.

Songs and music:

'There was an Old Lady who Lived in a Shoe'
'One, Two, Buckle my Shoe'
Paolo Nutini 'New Shoes'
Nancy Sinatra 'These Boots Are Made For Walking'
Elvis Presley 'Blue Suede Shoes'
K.C. and the Sunshine Band 'Boogie Shoes'
Brian Easdale 'The Red Shoes'
Sergei Prokofiev 'Cinderella Goes to the Ball' (from 'Cinderella Suite No.1')
Stevie Wonder 'I Wish' (from 'Happy Feet')

Taking it further

▶ Try a wellington boots dance. Help the children to put on their boots and stand in a circle. Play 'These Boots Are Made For Walking' and make some simple steps. Try stepping forwards and backwards in time to the beat. Stamp the boots. Bend down and stretch up.

▶ Read or tell the story of Cinderella. Act out the scene when the Prince comes to her house with the glass slipper. How will the ugly stepsisters react? Will the slipper fit onto Cinderella's foot?

Spring has sprung

Related themes: Spring, Growth, Minibeasts

What you need:

▶ Recorded music or access to YouTube – see 'Songs and music'
▶ 'Tapping tops' – pairs of lids from polish sprays or fabric softener bottles
▶ Yellow dusters

What you do:

Music makers

▶ Provide the children with pairs of 'tapping tops' to tap together. Show them how to make different sounds by tapping the open tops or the bottoms together.
▶ Encourage them to tap along to the beat as they sing this song to the tune of 'Did you ever see a Lassie?':

Can you tap the tops together,
Together, together?
Can you tap the tops together,
And keep to the beat?

Moving to music

1. Talk about 'spring cleaning' and why we might feel like cleaning when spring arrives.

2. Provide each child with a clean yellow duster. Ask them to try some cleaning moves!

3. Demonstrate how to hold the duster in one corner and swing it through the air from side to side. Try different levels – high, middle, low. Can they reach the cobweb in the corner of the room? Do they need to stand on tiptoe?

4. Ask the children to scrunch up the duster into a ball and try making some circular moves in front of them, as though polishing.

5. Play 'Spring Cleaning' by Fats Waller. Ask the children to listen to the song. When the solo piano starts playing, invite the children to try out some of their spring-cleaning moves with the music.

6. Divide the children into groups – some dusting up high, others polishing, some scrubbing the floor, others shaking the dusters. As the different instruments play solos, invite different groups to show off their spring-cleaning dances.

Games:

▶ Sing this song to the tune of 'Oh when the Saints':

Oh in the spring, it's time to clean,   x2
It's time to po-lish the windows,
Oh in the spring, it's time to clean.

▶ Ask the children to mime the spring-cleaning job as they sing. Can they reach up high and polish the top of the windows?

▶ Invite the children to mime a different spring-cleaning job such as mopping the floor, dusting the shelves, or scrubbing the step. Can the other children guess what they are doing and join in?

Songs and music:

'Mary Had a Little Lamb'
'Five Little Ducks'
'Daffy Down Dilly'
Frank Churchill 'Little April Shower' (from 'Bambi')
Antonio Vivaldi 'Spring' (from 'The Four Seasons')
Igor Stravinsky 'The Rite of Spring'
Frederick Delius 'On Hearing The First Cuckoo In Spring'
Hugh Masekela 'Grazing In The Grass'
Cat Stevens 'Morning Has Broken'
The Beatles 'Here Comes The Sun'
George Formby 'When I'm Cleaning Windows'
Fats Waller 'Spring Cleaning'

Taking it further

▶ Try some yoga poses related to spring. Ask the children to start by sitting cross-legged with their hands palms pressed together as though in prayer.

▶ Move to the butterfly pose – ask the children to put the soles of their feet together and move their hands to their heads, with their index fingers extended like antennae. Can the children bounce their knees gently like flapping wings and wiggle their index fingers? Exhale and move the hands slowly down.

▶ Try the frog pose. Ask the children to squat on the floor and balance on their toes. Place their hands down on the floor, look up and breathe in. As they breathe out, can they straighten their legs and lower their heads to their knees?

Summer sunshine

Related themes: Summer, Weather, Holidays

What you need:

▶ Recorded music or access to YouTube – see 'Songs and music'
▶ A collection of musical instruments
▶ Plastic bottles and a selection of materials
▶ Seaside buckets and spades, sun hats and sunglasses

What you do:

Music makers

▶ Go outside with a collection of musical instruments and make some loud music.
▶ Make some summer soundshakers. Use clear plastic bottles and fill with different summery materials such as sand, shells, pebbles and coloured water.

Moving to music

1. Ask the children to find a space. Can they travel around the room in different ways –walking, hopping, crawling, jumping, running, etc.?

2. Explain that they are now going to pretend that it's a hot summer day and they must move around slowly, as though the sun is beating down, the ground is burning hot, and they are feeling very hot and tired.

3. Play 'Adagio' from 'Summer' by Vivaldi. Can they move slowly around during the languid violin solo and stop and stand still each time the chords interrupt? These chords represent the 'furious swarm of flies and hornets'!

4. Try creating a beach dance. Provide the children with plastic buckets and spades, sun hats and sunglasses.

5. Children can stand in two lines wearing their sun hats and glasses. Ask them to step forwards and backwards while keeping the line straight.

6. Play 'Sunshine, Lollipops and Rainbows'. Ask one line to try tapping the beat on the buckets with the spades as the other line moves forwards and backwards.

7. Add other moves such as side steps and turns. Throw the hats in the air at the end!

Games:
▶ Try some traditional summer fête games with the children such as hoopla or quoits, skittles, sack race, egg and spoon, 'find the treasure on a map', 'guess the number of sweets in a jar' or even 'soak the teacher'!

Songs and music:

'The Sun Has Got His Hat On'
Cliff Richard 'Summer Holiday'
Joaquin Rodrigo 'Concierto de Aranjuez'
Claude Debussy 'Prélude à l'après-midi d'un Faune'
Astor Piazzolla 'Summer' (from 'The Four Seasons of Buenos Aires')
Antonio Vivaldi 'Summer' (from 'The Four Seasons')
Traditional 'Summer is i-cumen in'
Morecambe and Wise 'Bring Me Sunshine'
Lesley Gore 'Sunshine, Lollipops and Rainbows'
George Gershwin 'Summertime'
U2 'Beautiful Day'
Chubby Checker 'Let's Twist Again'
Arrow 'Feeling Hot Hot Hot'
Katrina and the Waves 'Walking on Sunshine'

Taking it further

▶ Play 'Let's Twist Again' or 'Feeling Hot, Hot, Hot'. Have a 'danceathon'. Who can keep twisting or dancing all through the song?

▶ Massage some flower petals into play dough for the children to model summer scenes and objects. Alternatively, for a multisensory experience, spray the dough with perfume or oils so it smells like flowers.

Superhero city

Related themes: Superheroes, All about me

What you need:

- Recorded music or access to YouTube – see 'Songs and music'
- Cardboard tubes
- Drum

What you do:

Music makers

- Listen to the 'Superman Theme'. Talk with the children about the instruments they can hear.
- Encourage the children to pretend to play along to the theme using junk trumpets made from cardboard tubes.
- Ask the children to make up a new superhero, such as 'Lightning Guy' or 'Magic Mountain'. Help the children to compose a theme or chant for their new character. What will the superpower be?

Moving to music

1. Many superheroes move very fast. Ask the children to practise moving at different speeds. Use a drumbeat to change the speed. How fast can the children (carefully!) travel around the room?

2. Play 'Superman Theme'. During the fanfare, invite the children to march around. When the orchestra comes in with the theme, ask them to move faster, like superheroes.

3. Talk about different ways that superheroes move such as flying, climbing, swimming, teleporting, leaping and so on.

4. Ask the children to each find a space in the room and give them time to try out these different ways of moving. They could try flying superhero style with one arm outstretched, pretending to climb upwards, wall-crawling like Spiderman, moving their arms as though swimming quickly, and taking giant leaps around the room. How could they demonstrate teleporting?

5. Organise the children into groups, each with a particular type of movement.

6. Play the 'Superhero Music' mix. Let each group perform and show others their ideas.

Games:

▶ Play a version of 'Beans', using different superheroes. Start with two contrasting characters such as Superman – fly around the room with one arm stretched out to the front and hand clenched in a fist; and Spiderman – climb around the room on all fours, with fingers held out like claws.

▶ Try adding some more heroes when the children are confident, such as the Hulk, Batman, Ironman, Wonderwoman and Catwoman. Use the children's own ideas to represent each character.

Songs and music:

John Williams 'Superman Theme'
Paul Webster and Robert Harris 'Spiderman Original Theme'
Danny Elfman 'Batman Theme'
'Original Batman TV Theme'
Fingathing 'Superhero Music' mix
Nintendo 'Super Mario Bros. Original Theme'
Electric Joy Ride 'Arcade Superhero'
Bonnie Tyler 'I Need a Hero'

Taking it further

▶ Make simple masks for the superheroes to wear. Cut out a basic shape and let the children decorate their own with a variety of collage materials.

▶ Make a list of superhero sounds – 'Boom!', 'Zap!', 'Pow!', 'Whizz!', 'Bam!' Show the children how to write these words in large capitals and then decorate them in a pop art or cartoon style with lots of layers of colours and shapes.

The flamboyant flypast

Related themes: Machines, Animals, Space, Travel

What you need:

▶ Recorded music or access to YouTube – see 'Songs and music'
▶ Balloons, saree or small parachute
▶ Paper to make folded airplanes

What you do:

Music makers

▶ Sit in a circle around a saree or parachute. Place some partially inflated balloons on the saree. Move the saree up and down so that the balloons float with it.
▶ Sing this song to the tune of 'Jack and Jill':
   Watch the balloons float up and down,
   Up and down together.
   Catch the balloons, float up and down,
   Whatever the weather.

Moving to music

1. Ask the children to find a space. Blow up a balloon and then slowly let the air out. Repeat and ask the children to use their bodies to pretend to grow bigger as the balloon inflates, and then shrink as the balloon deflates.

2. What happens if you blow up the balloon and then let go? Can the children rush around like the noisy deflating balloon? Play '1000 Airplanes on the Roof' or 'Up, Up and Away' as they move.

3. Talk about planes and how they move. Think about take off and landing, gliding, cruising, turbulence, turning, dipping wings, rotations, formation flying, etc.

4. Ask the children to find a space. Allow them time to travel around the room in different ways as though flying.

5. Play 'Flight of the Valkyries'. Let the children take turns to fly past doing different aerobatics.

6. Watch a video clip of the Red Arrows flying in formation. Ask the children to work in groups of four or five. Can they stand in a line of four and move across the room together? Ask them to try moving in a 'V' formation.

7. Play 'Those Magnificent Men in their Flying Machines' as the children move around in groups.

Games:

▶ Play 'No fly zone'. Ask the children to find a space in the room. When you shout out the name of something that flies – plane, rocket, hot air balloon, owl, bee, robin, butterfly, helicopter, etc. – they must pretend to fly in the appropriate way.

▶ If you shout out the name of something that doesn't fly – cow, car, bike, flower, dog, cat, train, etc. – they must stand still.

▶ The children who fly at the wrong time have to go and stand in the 'No fly zone'!

Songs and music:

Philip Glass '1000 Airplanes on the Roof'
Ron Goodwin 'Those Magnificent Men in their Flying Machines'
Norman Dello Joio 'Air Power'
Richard Wagner 'Flight of the Valkyries'
Karlheinz Stockhausen 'Helicopter String Quartet'
Frank Sinatra 'Come Fly With Me'
The 5th Dimension 'Up, Up and Away'
Richard M. Sherman and Robert B. Sherman 'Let's Go Fly a Kite'

Taking it further

▶ Sing 'Let's Go Fly a Kite' from 'Mary Poppins'. Go outside on a windy day and fly a kite.

▶ Show the children how to make simple folded paper aeroplanes. Organise a competition to find out which plane flies the furthest.

The rain dancers

Related themes: Weather, Spring, Growth, Water

What you need:

▶ Recorded music or access to YouTube – see 'Songs and music'
▶ Small children's umbrellas

I will need

What you do:

Music makers

▶ Ask a small group of the children to stand around the water tray. Provide a selection of metal trays, foil containers, sieves, colanders, funnels and plastic pots with holes punched into them. Invite the children to experiment with the sounds of the water. Which container makes the water sound most like rain?

▶ Now use rain sticks, maracas and other shakers to create rain sounds. Can the children organise the sounds into a sequence as the rain gets heavier?

Moving to music

1. Watch the clip of Gene Kelly dancing to 'Singing in the Rain'. Talk about how he uses his umbrella as a prop as he dances.

2. Invite the children to stand in a circle, each with a small closed umbrella. Start by showing them some simple moves such as walking forwards or backwards using the umbrella like a walking stick, or walking in a circle around it.

3. Can they stand behind the umbrella with both their hands on the handle and step to each side, tapping their heels and then toes?

4. Ask the children to move into two lines and open the umbrellas (remind them careful not to poke anybody with them). Encourage them to try lifting the umbrellas up behind their heads and walking along in a 'follow the leader' style.

5. Help the children practise holding the umbrellas upside down and spinning them around.

6. Can they think of any moves of their own?

7. Join all the moves together into a sequence to go with the song.

Games:

▶ Cut out some puddle shapes from newspaper, mirror plastic or silver paper. Place them randomly on the floor. Invite the children to walk around the room, jumping from puddle to puddle.

▶ Play any of the music from the 'Songs and music' section below and invite the children to dance around the puddles. When the music stops they must find a puddle to jump in quickly.

▶ Try this outside on a rainy day, wearing waterproof clothes, wellington boots and using real puddles!

Songs and music:

'Rain, Rain, Go Away'
'It's Raining, It's Pouring'
'I Hear Thunder'
Frank Churchill 'Little April Showers' (from 'Bambi')
Frédéric Chopin 'Raindrop Prelude'
Claude Debussy 'Estampes: Jardins Sous La Pluie'
Gene Kelly 'Singing in the Rain'
B.J. Thomas 'Raindrops Keep Falling On My Head'

Taking it further

▶ Try this yoga rainbow pose: kneel on the floor and raise both hands above the head. Drop one arm down, stretch, exhale and arch the other arm over the head like a rainbow. Ask the children to think of the colours of the rainbow. Repeat using opposite arms.

▶ Paint an instant rainbow. Put seven blobs of different colours in a row on one side of the paper. Place a cardboard tube or ruler on the paint and move it slowly round in a semi-circular curve.

The three bears jive

Related themes: Bears, Animals, Traditional tales, Dynamics

What you need:

▶ Recorded music or access to YouTube – see 'Songs and music'
▶ A selection of musical instruments
▶ Three teddy bears of different sizes

I will need

What you do:

Music makers

▶ Talk to the children about dynamics (loud/quiet). Sit in a circle and place an instrument in front of each child. On your signal, ask the children to pick up their instrument and make a sound. Use a simple gesture such as closed fists to show them when to stop.

▶ Introduce the children to the three bears. Baby Bear likes silence – ask the children to pick up the instruments without making a sound. Keep trying until they can do this in silence. Mummy Bear likes quiet sounds – go around the circle and invite each child to make a quiet sound. Daddy Bear likes loud sounds – go around the circle and invite each child to make a loud sound.

Moving to music

1. Try some simple hand jiving – clapping hands, sliding hands one over the other, hammering fists on top of each other, tapping elbows with palms, hitch-hiking thumbs over shoulders.
2. Can they make up any new moves to include in the hand jives?
3. Devise a simple sequence of moves and let the children try them out as they listen to 'In The Mood'.

4. Play 'The Wild Bears'. Talk to the children about how they imagine the bears would dance to this music. It is very fast and loud.

5. Ask the children to practise moving like bears: they should try moving on all fours, slowly walking around, rolling on their backs to scratch an itch, and rearing up on their back legs to try and scare away other bears!

6. Ask the children to each choose a partner to dance with. When the music starts, they should walk around each other on all fours. During the oboe solo, the bears can walk away from each other, then approach the other bear again but a bit more aggressively. When the fast tune returns they could rise up on their 'hind' legs and pretend to box. End with a bear hug!

Games:

▶ Sit in a circle and invite one child to curl up in the middle, pretending to be Daddy Bear fast asleep. Make sure the child closes their eyes and covers their face. Place a small shaker or set of bells behind the child.

▶ Invite another child to creep into the circle and take the instrument from behind Daddy Bear without 'waking him up'/ without the child noticing. How quiet can they be?

Songs and music:

'When Goldilocks went to the House of the Bears'
'The Bear Went Over The Mountain'
Henry Hall 'The Teddy Bears' Picnic'
'Round and Round the Garden'
'Teddy Bear, Teddy Bear, Touch Your Nose'
Edward Elgar 'The Wild Bears'
Bill Haley 'Shake, Rattle and Roll'
The Bee Gees 'Jive Talkin''
Glenn Miller 'In The Mood'

Taking it further

▶ Sing the song 'The Bear Went Over The Mountain' and ask the children to walk round in a circle to the slow beat of the drum. Change the word 'went' to 'walked'. Then change the beat of the drum to match these other words: 'ran' (fast), 'jumped' (slow), 'hopped' (slow), 'skipped' (jumpy), 'crawled' (very slow), 'danced' (jumpy), and so on.

▶ Try some paw printing. Provide shallow trays full of thick finger paint. Use the thumb print as the centre or pad of the paw and the index finger as the four toes. Can the children print a bear trail for others to follow?

Top of the hat parade

Related themes: Hats, Clothes, All about me

What you need:

▶ Recorded music or access to YouTube – see 'Songs and music'
▶ A selection of gloves, mittens and socks
▶ Saree or small parachute
▶ Different-coloured scarves
▶ A hat with a set of cards in it – each card naming an item of clothing

What you do:

Music makers

▶ Try some echo clapping. Clap a simple rhythm and invite the children to copy after you. Show them how to clap with loud hand claps. Can they also echo the rhythm quietly, using two-finger tapping?

▶ Provide a pair of gloves or mittens for each child. Ask them to echo clap some rhythms while wearing the gloves.

▶ Roll the pairs of gloves or socks into balls and place them on a saree or parachute. Invite the children to sit in a circle and hold the edges of the saree. Move it up and down as you sing this song to the tune of 'Here We Go Round The Mulberry Bush':

The gloves/socks are jumping up and down,
Up and down, up and down,
The gloves/socks are jumping up and down,
In the washing machine.

Moving to music

1. Provide each child with a scarf. Ask them to hold it at the two top corners and let it hang down as though on the washing line. The children should try blowing on the scarves to make them move. Can they move the scarves gently forwards and backwards, like the wind blows the washing?

2. What will happen when the wind blows more strongly? The scarves will be blown off the line. Ask the children to now hold just one corner of the scarf and make it move around in circles. Show the children how to scrunch up the scarves and throw them into the air.

3. Play 'The Storm' (from the 'William Tell Overture'). As the storm grows and the wind gets more fierce, ask the children to move the scarves more and more vigorously. What will happen to all the washing on the line?

4. Now focus on a different article of clothing: hats. Provide each child with a hat. They should practise standing up tall wearing the hat, and then taking it off and holding it high above the head and then out to the front.

5. Play 'Mexican Hat Dance'. The music is divided into lots of different sections. Split the children into groups of four, allocate each group a section of music and help each group to think of actions for their musical segment. Use a variety of movements such as stamping, clapping, and moving their hats!

6. Ask the children to stand in four straight lines. The front line can perform the movement they have chosen for the first section, then the second line, and so on.

Games:

▶ Ask the children to sit in a circle. Pass a hat around the ring, with the clothes cards inside. Play any music from the 'Songs and music' section below.

▶ When the music stops, ask the child holding the hat to take out a card. Can they mime putting on the item of clothing named on the card, such as socks, hat, trousers, jumper, etc., for the others to guess?

Songs and music:

'The Sun Has Got His Hat On'
'Diddle Diddle Dumpling'
'Down In The Jungle'
Gioachino Rossini 'William Tell Overture - The Storm'

'The Mexican Hat Dance' ('El Jarabe Tapatio')

Stanley Holloway 'Where Did You Get That Hat?'

Fred Astaire 'Top Hat, White Tie and Tails'

Andrew Lloyd Webber 'Joseph's Coat', (from 'Joseph and the Amazing Technicolour Dreamcoat')

The Kinks 'Dedicated Follower of Fashion'

Brian Hyland 'Itsy Bitsy Teenie Weenie Yellow Polka Dot Bikini'

Taking it further

▶ Provide lots of collage materials and ask the children to design some fancy hats. Organise a hat parade and help them to walk in time to one of the songs about hats (see 'Songs and music') and model their creations.

Tracking trains

Related themes: Trains, Transport, Journeys, Tempo

What you need:

▶ Recorded music or access to YouTube – see 'Songs and music'
▶ Pairs of claves, enough for each child
▶ Sandpaper blocks
▶ Tambourine

What you do:

Music makers

▶ Introduce the term 'tempo' and talk about different speeds – fast and slow. Choose a song from the 'Songs and music' section and invite the children to tap along to the beat on their knees.
▶ Try tapping claves or scraping sand paper blocks to the beat of the music.
▶ Ask the children to make up some train rhythms using the claves and sand paper blocks. Try scrape, scrape, tap tap, scrape. Repeat the pattern over and over.

Moving to music

1. Play 'Different Trains'. What sounds can the children hear besides the musical instruments? A train station is a busy, bustling place, full of the sounds of trains, people and announcements. Together, make a list of words or phrases about trains.

2. Divide the children into four or five small groups. Give each group a different word or phrase to chant over the music.

3. Ask each group to form a train by standing in a line with their hands on each other's shoulders or waists. Can they move along as a unit, following the leader or train driver?

4. Play the music again and let them move around and chant, at the same time taking care not to bump into another train!

5. Play 'Pacific 231' or 'Little Train of Caipira'. Talk about changes to the tempo of the music. Let the children choose a simple movement to represent the train, e.g. walking around as they move their hands around like wheels. Can they keep this going as they react to the changes in tempo? What happens when the train gets faster? Or crashes?

Games:

▶ Ask the children to stand in a circle and begin to walk around in a clockwise direction. On an agreed signal, such as one tap on a tambourine, they must all change direction.

▶ When the children are confident, introduce these challenges: two taps on a tambourine means go faster; three taps indicates slow motion.

Songs and music:

'Engine, Engine, Number Nine'
'Down at the Station'
The Seekers 'Morningtown Ride'
'The Runaway Train'
Arthur Honegger 'Pacific 231'
Heitor Villa-Lobos 'Little Train of Caipira'
Eduard Strauss 'Bahn Frei! Polka Schnell'
Glenn Miller 'Chattanooga Choo Choo'
Steve Reich 'Different Trains (Part 1)'
R.E.M. 'Driver 8'
Doobie Brothers 'Long Train Running'
The O'Jays 'Love Train'
Jimmie Rodgers 'Train Whistle Blues'

Taking it further

▶ Go outside and draw lots of sets of parallel train tracks using different coloured playground chalk. The children must stay inside the tracks for their train.

▶ Try some printing with plastic vehicles. Use plastic trains and cars. Show the children how to drive the vehicles in shallow paint trays and then along long strips of paper to create tyre tracks.

Traditional telling tales

Related themes: Traditional tales, Tempo, Food

What you need:

▶ Recorded music or access to YouTube – see 'Songs and music'
▶ A selection of musical instruments
▶ Two picture cards – a bumblebee and a snail
▶ A gingerbread man finger puppet or cardboard cut-out

What you do:

Music makers

▶ Talk about tempo (fast/slow). Ask the children to sing a well-known song twice, at different tempos.

▶ Show them two contrasting picture cards representing fast and slow – the bee and the snail.

▶ Sit the children in a circle and place an instrument in front of each child. Can they play their instrument 'fast' or 'slow' according to which picture card you are holding up?

Moving to music

1. Play 'Little Red Riding Hood'. What do the children think is happening in the music? Can they hear the wolf's low, growling movements? And Red Riding Hood's higher, faster movements? Perhaps the wolf is tracking Red Riding Hood as she walks through the wood to her Grandmother's house.

2. Ask each child to choose a partner and find a space in the room. Let them take turns at playing the parts of the wolf and the girl. How will they move in character? Play an excerpt of the music and let them work together.

3. Tell the traditional story of The Gingerbread Man, using the puppet as a visual aid. Encourage the children to join in the chant: 'Run, run, as fast as you can – you can't catch me, I'm the Gingerbread Man!'

4. Act out the story together. Each time the Gingerbread Man has to run, play 'Rondo' or 'Plink, Plank, Plunk'. How fast can the children run?

5. Just before he comes to his nasty end, make up a special Gingerbread Man dance. Play 'Sweet Gingerbread Man'. Watch it performed by The Muppets.

6. Ask each child to stand in a space. Help them to step from side to side in time to the beat and clap their hands. Develop this: shrug shoulders, tap knees, clap hands with a partner, and join arms and dance with a partner in a circle.

Games:

▶ Play 'Pavane of the Sleeping Beauty'. Ask the children to find a place to lie down and play 'sleeping lions' while they listen to the music. Anybody that you see move is 'out'.

Songs and music:

'When Goldilocks Went To The House Of The Bears'

Henry Hall 'Who's Afraid Of The Big Bad Wolf?'

Maurice Ravel 'Pavane of the Sleeping Beauty'

Pyotr Ilyich Tchaikovsky 'Sleeping Beauty Waltz'

David Allenby 'Sweet Gingerbread Man'

Sergei Rachmaninoff 'Etudes Tableaux Op.39: Little Red Riding Hood'

Wolfgang Amadeus Mozart 'Horn Concerto No. 4 Rondo'

Leroy Anderson 'Plink, Plank, Plunk'

Charles Williams 'The Devil's Galop'

Taking it further

▶ Vote for the group's favourite traditional tale, act it out and write some incidental music to accompany the action. Use any of the music from 'Songs and music' for inspiration.

▶ Bake some gingerbread men biscuits and share for snack.

Traffic jams

Related themes: Cars, Transport, Journeys

What you need:

▶ Recorded music or access to YouTube – see 'Songs and music'
▶ A selection of musical instruments
▶ A set of cards showing the traffic lights sequence - red, red and orange, green, orange, back to red
▶ Tambourines
▶ Hula hoops

What you do:

Music makers

▶ Ask the children to sit in a circle and place a different musical instrument in front of each child. Practise stopping and starting the instrument following a conductor – open hands to start, close fists to stop.

▶ Talk about the sequence of traffic light colours. Use the cards to help the children play the instruments: stop, get ready, play, slow down, and repeat. You may wish to simplify this to 'stop, get ready, play' until they get the hang of it.

▶ Show the children how to play slowly. Remind them that slowly is not the same as quietly!

Moving to music

1. Ask the children to find a space. Provide each child with a tambourine to use as a steering wheel and invite them to move around taking care not to bump into each other. Use the traffic light cards to stop and start the vehicles (see 'Music makers').

2. Ask each child to work with a partner and a hula hoop. Help the children to stand with their partner inside a hoop. One is the passenger, holding onto the hula hoop at the sides. The other is the driver and stands in front, holding onto the front of the hoop.

3. Play 'Cars' or 'Route 66'. Can the children coordinate their moves safely as they drive around the space? What happens if there is a traffic jam?

4. Play 'An American in Paris'. Can the children hear the rushing cars, their horns (french horns and car horns) honking as they pass by? Can they hear the horses trotting (woodblocks) amongst the traffic? And people rushing about their business (xylophones)?

5. Divide the children into three groups – 'cars', 'horses' and 'people'. Devise different ways of moving for each group. Ask them to move around and respond to the musical sound effects.

Games:

▶ Play 'Bumper cars'. Each child has their own hoop, which becomes their car. The hoop defines their own space and they must be careful not to bump into anybody else.

▶ Children should find a space and start their engines! Suggest lots of different movements for the cars – drive forwards, backwards, slowly uphill, fast downhill, over a bumpy road, stuck in a traffic jam, right turn, turn left, break down, crash, park, and so on.

Songs and music:

George Gershwin 'An American in Paris'
Gary Numan 'Cars'
robert Sherman 'Chitty Chitty Bang Bang Theme Song'
Willie Nelson 'On the Road Again'
Beach Boys 'Little Deuce Coupe'
Chuck Berry 'Riding Along In My Automobile'
John Mayer 'Route 66'

Taking it further

▶ Let the children enjoy some races on sit-and-ride toys and tricycles. Draw chalk routes on the playground for the children to drive along.

▶ Make cardboard tube racing cars. Paint a small cardboard tube and cut out a square from the top for a small play figure to fit inside. Punch two holes in each side of the tube, a way apart, and in four plastic milk-bottle tops using a small nail. Push a cocktail stick through front and back and attach the wheels onto the sticks using Blu-Tack.

Waving water

Related themes: Water, Weather, Transport, Journeys

What you need:

► Recorded music or access to YouTube – see 'Songs and music'
► Five glass bottles and a jug of coloured water
► Blue/green scarves, or lengths of netting tied to curtain rings
► A large loop of elastic rope
► Small buckets, brushes and brooms

What you do:

Music makers

► Place five glass milk bottles in a line and fill them with different amounts of coloured water (use food colouring). Invite the children to tap the bottles gently and listen to the different sounds. Work with the children to arrange the bottles in order of pitch, from low to high. Can they make up a tune or musical pattern using the bottles?

► Sing this song to the tune of 'Ten green bottles':

Five glass bottles, standing in a line   x2
Tap one bottle and listen to it chime,
Five glass bottles, standing in a line.

Moving to music

1. Provide each child with a scarf, or a length of netting tied to a small ring. Ask them to find a space to sit.

2. How many different ways can they move the scarves or lengths of netting? Invite them to wave the material from side to side in front of them, over their head, behind them, in spirals, and so on.

3. Repeat with the children standing. Can they make the scarves ripple like waves, or flow like water falls? Invite them to demonstrate their ideas to each other.

4. Play 'Le Onde'. Let the children use their bodies and the scarves to move like the waves as they listen.

5. Ask the children to choose a partner to work with. Sit opposite each other, hold hands and sing 'Row, Row, Row the Boat' as they rock gently forwards and backwards.

6. Play 'Barcarolle'. During the introduction, ask the children to walk around the room and find a new partner to sit with. When the tune starts, can they rock their boats in time to the rocking beat of the music?

7. Try a yoga 'double boat' pose. Children sit opposite each other with their knees bent and big toes touching. Ask them to lean forward and hold hands. They should try lifting one leg and pressing the soles of their feet together, exhaling and then trying the other side.

8. As a challenge, ask them to lift both feet and press the soles together and rock back and forth. Can they move in time to the music while holding the pose?

Games:

▶ Sit in a circle with a loop of elasticated rope in the middle, and ask the children to hold onto the rope with both hands. Try moving the rope into the middle of circle and out again, as though rowing.

▶ Sing this song to the tune of 'The Farmer's in his Den' and let the children take it in turns to choose friends one by one to fill the boat:

(Child's name) in his boat, x2
Hey ho, here we row.
(Child's name) in his boat.

Songs and music:

'Row, Row, Row The Boat'
'A Sailor Went To Sea'
'The Big Ship Sails'
Jacques Offenbach 'Barcarolle'
Felix Mendelssohn 'Hebrides Overture'
Claude Debussy 'La Mer'

84

Henry Wood 'The Sailor's Hornpipe'
Ludovico Einaudi 'Le Onde' ('The Waves')
Camille Saint-Saëns 'The Carnival of the Animals: Aquarium'
Maurice Ravel 'Jeux d'eau'
Franz Schubert 'The Trout'
Paul Abraham Dukas 'The Sorcerer's Apprentice' (from 'Fantasia')
Alan Menken 'Under the Sea' (from 'The Little Mermaid')
Rod Stewart 'Sailing'
Enya 'Orinoco Flow'

Taking it further

▶ Watch the clip of 'The Sorcerer's Apprentice' from 'Fantasia'. Provide small brushes, buckets and brooms and help the children to devise their own watery dance. Try this sequence: tap, sweep, sweep, sweep. Bang the buckets on the floor in time to the beat.

▶ Try some magic underwater painting. Provide the children with white candles or wax crayons to draw wavy lines and fishes on to a large piece of paper. Apply a thin blue paint wash all over the paper and watch the waves and fish emerge.

Winter wonderland

Related themes: Winter wonderland

What you need:

▶ Recorded music or access to YouTube – see 'Songs and music'
▶ A selection of metal percussion instruments
▶ Short sticks with silver tinsel attached
▶ Small squares of white netting
▶ Large white sheet and some white polystyrene balls

What you do:

Music makers

▶ Provide a collection of metal instruments such as triangles, jingle bells, Indian bells, cow bells, glockenspiels and chime bars.

▶ Add some junk metal sounds such as biscuit tins, saucepan lids, metal spoons or forks, metal piping, sieves, whisks, and more – if possible, suspended on a metal frame.

▶ Let the children explore the delicate, tinkling, tapping, rattly, bright sounds to create their own musical winter wonderland.

Moving to music

1. Play 'The Snow is Dancing'. Invite the children to sit in a circle and use their hands to make snowflakes, fluttering and dancing in the air as they listen.

2. Ask them to find a space and make snowflake shapes with their whole body. Can they make every finger and toe, hand and foot, and arm and leg 'spikey'?

3. Play the music again and encourage them to move around like snowflakes, darting around the space on tiptoe.

4. Provide the children with tinsel sticks or white net scarves and let them add these to the snowflakes dance.

5. Play 'Footsteps in the Snow' and talk about the contrast between the two pieces.

6. Now the children have to move around pretending to tread in heavy, deep snow, as if leaving footprints as they go. Ask them to each work with a partner and play the music again. One child must walk ahead, pretending to carefully make footprints, and the other must follow and try to place their feet in the same places, as though treading in the same footprints.

Games:

▶ Sit in a circle and ask the children to hold onto the edge of a large white sheet. Move the sheet up and down together, like a parachute.

▶ Place one white ball on the sheet and let it roll around as you lift the sheet up and down. Try singing this song as you move to the tune of 'Skip to my Loo':

One little snowball rolling around,   x3
Called for another to join in.

▶ Add more snowballs and repeat the song, increasing the numbers until you reach 'lots of snowballs rolling around'! Can the children use the sheet to flick the snowballs into the air so they jump up and down?

Songs and music:

Maurice Jarre 'Lara's Theme' (from 'Dr. Zhivago')
Howard Blake 'Walking in the Air'
Claude Debussy 'Footsteps in the Snow'
Claude Debussy 'The Snow is Dancing'
Frederick Delius 'Sleigh Ride'
'Do You Want to Build A Snowman?' (from 'Frozen')
Felix Bernard 'Winter Wonderland'
Sigur Ros 'Cold'

Taking it further

▶ Make snowflakes from white art straws, cotton wool, glitter, sequins, pompoms, etc. Hang them up around the setting as decorations.

The Little Books Club

There is always something in Little Books to help and inspire you. Packed full of lovely ideas, Little Books meet the need for exciting and practical activities that are fun to do, address the Early Learning Goals and can be followed in most settings. Everyone is a winner!

We publish 5 new Little Books a year. Little Books Club members receive each of these 5 books as soon as they are published for a reduced price. The subscription cost is £29.99 – a one off payment that buys the 5 new books for £4.99 instead of £8.99 each.

In addition to this, Little Books Club Members receive:
- Free postage and packing on anything ordered from the Featherstone catalogue
- A 15% discount voucher upon joining which can be used to buy any number of books from the Featherstone catalogue
- Members price of £4.99 on any additional Little Book purchased
- A regular, free newsletter dealing with club news, special offers and aspects of Early Years curriculum and practice
- All new Little Books on approval - return in good condition within 30 days and we'll refund the cost to your club account

Call 020 7458 0200 or email: littlebooks@bloomsbury.com for an enrolment pack. Or download an application form from our website:
www.bloomsbury.com